Creative Grace

American University Studies

Series VII
Theology and Religion
Vol. 152

PETER LANG
New York • San Francisco • Bern • Baltimore
Frankfurt am Main • Berlin • Wien • Paris

Stephen F. Dintaman

Creative Grace

Faith and History
in the
Theology of Adolf Schlatter

PETER LANG
New York • San Francisco • Bern • Baltimore
Frankfurt am Main • Berlin • Wien • Paris

Library of Congress Cataloging-in-Publication Data

Dintaman, Stephen F.
    Creative grace: faith and history in the theology of Adolf Schlatter /
Stephen F. Dintaman.
        p.   cm. — (American university studies. Series VII, Theology and
religion; vol. 152)
    Includes bibliographical references.
    1. Schlatter, Adolf von, 1852–1938. 2. Bible. N.T.—Criticism,
interpretation, etc.—History—19th century. 3. Bible. N.T.—Criticism,
interpretation, etc.—History—20th century. 4. Theology—19th century.
5. Theology—20th century. 6. Grace (Theology)—History of doctrines.
I. Title. II. Series.
BS2351.S3D56   1993   241'.0404'092—dc20   93-29664
ISBN 0-8204-2118-9   CIP
ISSN 0740-0446

Die Deutsche Bibliothek-CIP-Einheitsaufnahme

Dintaman, Stephen F.:
Creative grace: faith and history in the theology of Adolf Schlatter/ Stephen F.
Dintaman. - New York; Berlin; Bern; Frankfurt/M.; Paris; Wien: Lang, 1993
   (American university studies: Ser. 7, Theology and religion; Vol. 152)
   ISBN 0-8204-2118-9
NE: American university studies / 07

The paper in this book meets the guidelines for permanence and durability of
the Committee on Production Guidelines for Book Longevity of the
Council on Library Resources.

Printed in the United States of America.

Dedicated to

Betsy Halteman Dintaman

My constant companion in the joys and struggles of life

ACKNOWLEDGEMENTS

The original idea for a dissertation on the theology of Adolf Schlatter came from a discussion with Prof. Peter Stuhlmacher in the Summer of 1978. I had appreciated his work in *Historical Criticism and Theological Interpretation of Scripture* (Philadelphia: Fortress Press, 1977), and he graciously shared his time and suggestions with me when I visited him at his home in Tübingen. It was he who first suggested that the study of Schlatter could provide a fruitful opportunity to explore the issue of faith and history.

Thanks to a stipend from the Deutsche Akademische Austausch Dienst, I was able to spend the the Fall Semester of 1980 in Tübingen, and use both the University library, and the library of the Protestant Faculty. I was also able to take advantage of the Schlatter Archive in nearby Stuttgart. Prof. Stuhlmacher gave me good counsel during this time. I especially owe an immense debt of gratitude to Dr. Hans Stroh, then retired and living in nearby Reutlingen. Dr. Stroh had at one time served as a student assistant to Prof. Schlatter and had the whole of Schlatter's thought and life at his command. He spent many days hearing out my ideas and guiding me into several new ones. His knowledge and generosity has greatly enriched my understanding of Schlatter. Dr. Stroh's death in 1989 created a deep sense of loss among the circle of friends and scholars who over the years had drawn on his broad knowledge of Schlatter.

I am also indebted to my dissertation committee at Princeton Theological Seminary for their patience and interest in my work on Schlatter. My chairman, Dr. David Willis-Watkins, along with Dr. Daniel Migliore and Dr. J.C. Beker, helped focus and direct my efforts to a successful completion of the first edition of this work for which I was awarded my Ph.D. in Systematic Theology (*cum laude*) by Princeton Theological Seminary.

More recently it has been my good fortune to work with Dr. Werner Neuer, a young German scholar (we were born in the same month!) who has made a career of Schlatter research. Dr. Neuer's recent short biography of

Schlatter (*Adolf Schlatter*, Wuppertal: R. Brockhaus Verlag, 1988.), anticipates an exhaustive Schlatter biography that he is now working on under the auspices of the Schlatter Foundation. His research and numerous publications clearly establish him as the leading Schlatter research scholar on the scene today. Dr. Neuer's numerous corrections, suggestions and encouragements added greatly to my original work as I prepared it for this publication.

While this has been an academic project, academics can never be separated from life. I also want to express my special debt to my wife, Betsy Halteman Dintaman, and our children, Abram and Anna, who helped give me a family life that kept my academic interests and pursuits in proper perspective.

TABLE OF CONTENTS

FOREWORD

The theological work and influence of Adolf Schlatter is one of the great enigmas of 20th century theology. Here is a man who is regarded by many as the one of the most original and significant theologians of his time, and yet his voluminous writings were never interpreted into English. Theologians as diverse as Rudolf Bultmann, Karl Barth, Peter Stuhlmacher, Ernst Käsemann and Ernst Fuchs have expressed deep appreciation and respect for his work, yet no clearly identifiable Schlatter school has existed throughout this century.

But there are signs of change in this regard. The last few years have seen the emergence of some significant scholarly work that presents Schlatter in a deeply sympathetic manner. Perhaps this begins with Peter Stuhlmacher's, *Historical Criticism and the Theological Interpretation of Scripture* (Fortress Press: Philadelphia, 1977), in which he acknowledges Schlatter's work as a starting point for his own openly confessional approach to the interpretation of scripture.

In the past few years several others have done significant work that helps us recover an awareness of who Schlatter was and what his possible significance for theology might be. A collection of essays edited by Klaus Bockmühl and entitled, *Die Aktualität der Theologie Adolf Schlatters* (Giessen/Basel: Brunnen Verlag, 1988), was released in 1988, the 50th anniversary of Schlatter's death. This book brings together the work of several younger German scholars who understand the uniqueness of Schlatter and are finding significant ways to make his voice heard in contemporary theological discussions. (See my 'Selected Bibliography', p.178, for authors and titles of specific essays.)

In particular, Dr. Werner Neuer has emerged as a tireless Schlatter researcher and advocate. Dr. Neuer's dissertation, *Dogmatik und Ethik bei Adolf Schlatter* (Giessen\Basel: Brunnen Verlag, 1986), and particularly his short biography, *Adolf Schlatter* (Wuppertal: R. Brockhaus Verlag, 1988), plus numerous shorter periodical articles, makes a wealth of detail about Schlatter's life and thought thoroughly accessible to the contemporary theologian interested in getting to know this famous, though still elusive, seminal theologian.

At least one American writer has done significant work that suggests the potential that lies in Schlatter's work. Edgar McKnight, in his book *Post-Modern Use of the Bible* (Nashville: Abingdon Press, 1988) shows how Stuhlmacher has taken and developed Schlatter as a model for a post-modern hermeneutic of scripture. Though his treatment of Schlatter is brief and merely suggestive, it shows sensitive insight into what Schlatter was up to in his own time, and at least suggests the potentiality that lies largely forgotten in his writings.

My work is the first book length discussion of Schlatter published in English. My hope is that it will provide the reader with some sense of the depth and breadth of this man's thought, and perhaps spark others to their own further research. While no work can cover the breadth of Schlatter's scholarly production, I do believe that by focusing on the question of faith and history, this work will lead readers to what is clearly the central focus and concern of his work.

Throughout the 20th century Schlatter has been largely ignored because his exegetical work was widely regarded as naive or pre-critical. Certainly in his own time period (1852–1938) it was the passion for scientific method that dominated biblical studies. While Schlatter was appreciated by many church people of a more conservative stripe, perhaps the times were not yet ready for his powerful, probing criticisms of the hidden dogmas that lay behind the historical methods of that period. Though many contemporary thinkers have put forward various criticisms of 19th century historicism, none are more original or penetrating than those Schlatter developed almost a century ago.

Today, we would call Schlatter's critique of the hegemony of narrowly defined canons of scientific methodology, 'post-modern'. The only problem is he was 'post-modern' while the fascination with modernity and its certain scientific methods was still at its full flower. If I were to look for a term that would dramatically highlight Schlatter's historical significiance and relevance for theology at the end of the 20th century, I would label him as the great 'proto-narrative' theologian of the late 19th and early 20th centuries.

My sole hope for this book is that it will make Schlatter's thought more accessible so that he may become a significant discussion partner for those theologians who believe that at times the way into the future is to recover aspects of our past.

–Stephen F. Dintaman
Eastern Mennonite College
Harrisonburg, VA

Creative Grace

Chapter I

A BIOGRAPHICAL INTRODUCTION

After several years of studying the career and work of Adolf Schlatter I am keenly aware that he is a virtual unknown except among a small coterie of bible scholars and theologians. Even among this elite group he is known primarily as a footnote in the works of Bultmann or Käsemann, or Brunner or Barth. The predominant knowledge most scholars have of Schlatter is a vague impression of a prolific New Testament scholar whose significance in a prior era has been eclipsed by the next generations of scholarship much as the steam engine has been eclipsed by internal combustion. He is regarded primarily as a workhorse exegete and instructor of pastors, but his name is usually not associated with any major contribution to the formation of 20th century biblical studies or theology.

In Germany the situation is in some respects quite different. Schlatter is well known by the current generation of university professors and senior pastors. Many studied with him or were students when he was regarded as a major theological power in German-speaking scholarship. His work continues to be read and utilized. But his writings are more often seen as having practical use in sermon preparation than as a major constructive theological method or option. But the careful reader of some significant New Testament scholarship can pick up hints of another aspect of Schlatter. Bultmann refers to him as a major milestone in the emergence of New Testament theology as a discipline. In fact, in his brief survey of the history of New Testament theology as a discipline in his *Theology of the New Testament*, Bultmann gives far more attention to Schlatter than to any other figure. One could even deduce from some of his comments that Bultmann took Schlatter as a major exemplar for his own program of New Testament hermeneutics.[1] Ernst Käsemann gives occasional suggestions of Schlatter's significance for the discipline and for some of his own creative work.[2] More recently Peter Stuhlmacher has done a great deal to recover the memory of Schlatter's work and to suggest its fruitfulness for contemporary discussions of hermeneutics.[3] Later in this biographical introduction we will attempt to summarize the lines of Schlatter's influence on biblical studies and theology, but first let us look briefly at his life and career.

Schlatter's Life and Career

Adolf Schlatter was born in Switzerland in 1852. His students reported that he carried a Swiss accent with him throughout his life that made his lectures difficult to follow. His parents, Stephan and Wilhelmine Schlatter, were residents of St. Gallen, and it is here that Adolf lived and was formed until he left for the university at age 19. His parents were very devout believers, and he speaks of them and of his childhood home as a island of light and love. He says in his autobiographical, *Rückblick auf meine Lebensarbeit*, that his parents not only gave him Christian instruction and guidance, but that he learned from them, "how a life under God's direction is lived".[4] One fascinating detail from his home life is the fact that his parents were members of quite different confessions. His mother was a member and devout participant of the local Reformed church, an official

*Translator's note: All translations of Schlatter's writings are the work of the author, except where I quote from Schlatter's "The Theology of the New Testament and Dogmatics", which was translated by Robert Morgan in *The Nature of New Testament Theology*, ed. Robert Morgan, Studies in Biblical Theology II, 25, and the extended quote from Ernst Käsemann (see pp. 13-14 following) which is taken from his, *New Testament Questions of Today*, translated by W.J. Montague (Philadelphia: Fortress Press, 1969).

state church in Switzerland. His father, however, separated himself from the state church and was a member of a voluntary "community of Jesus". In fact, his father was so strongly opposed to the state church, that he did not even attend his son's ordination to the pastorate. Yet the young Adolf observed that this confessional difference between his parents was no hindrance to their love and fellowship because both were devoted to Jesus and the scriptures and lived a life characterized by love. Adolf also learned from his father a critical perspective on the Reformation and the theology of the reformers that stayed with him throughout his career. He reports that he received from his father the impulse "to complete the Reformation".[5]

In fact, Schlatter reports that the "deepest and holiest" impulse that lay behind his theological work grew out of his father's criticism of the Reformation.[6] While his conflict with a scientific historical method used to attack Christian faith is the most obvious impulse behind his work, Schlatter himself at least saw this Reformation critique as more fundamental. The reformers, he came to see, did not attack the message of the gospel itself but the Reformation failed in that it did not lead to "the formation of christian community".[7] Instead it had replaced the medieval priesthood with another religious institution, that of the evangelical pastorate. It left the church much as it found it; a passive flock receiving religious services from a clerical institution. In as much as it did not create a new community of love and service it failed to carry through on the creative effects that proceed from Jesus. Schlatter will go so far as to write at one point:

> How can the church once again gain free access to the New Testament?
> To accomplish that I regard the criticism of the Reformation, especially
> Luther, to be essential. [8]

In his *Gymnasium* studies Schlatter excelled in philology, especially enjoying the study of Greek. He was deeply impressed by his language instructor, but also encountered in him a conflict that characterized his early studies. His instructor, a Catholic, was an advocate of Kantian philosophy and rejected many biblical ideas that were held sacred in the Schlatter home. Encouraged by his parents to pursue theological studies, Adolf reports that on one occasion he announced he would not study theology because university studies would damage his faith. A sharp rebuke from his sister made a deep impression on him and showed him that his fear of university studies was not an expression of faith. Schlatter writes that in effect,... "my decision to study theology was my conversion."[9]

Schlatter began his university studies at Basel in 1871. He was most intrigued by his philosophical studies and his most influential professor was a history of philosophy instructor, Karl Steffensen. Schlatter learned from the study of the history of philosophy that ideas emerge out of a complex set of historical relationships, so that... "even ideas have a history." He reports that, "Through Steffensen 'pure reason' died for me as I came to see how ideas arose out of historical processes."[10] He felt that through these studies he had been freed from the burden of the Greek heritage that dominates so much of intellectual life. Much of his later work can be seen as an attempt to consistently carry through this early insight into the historicity of reason.

He also reports hearing Nietzsche lecture but he was repulsed by his arrogance and disdain toward students. He reports that all he learned from observing Nietzsche is that when one forsakes love one also destroys the capacity for intellectual understanding.[11] He heard Burckhardt lecture on the history of culture and was impressed with his learning and insight. He also heard lectures in the New Testament, but reported that, "The text never came to life for me; only the exegetes spoke."

He continued his studies at Tübingen where he took a special interest in the lectures of Johannes Tobias Beck. What impressed him about Beck was his originality, and the way life and scholarship were combined in his teaching. Beck did not speak of hypotheses and theories but about what he confessed and believed. In that Beck's intellectual work was a part of his "life-act", and that he taught with joy and conviction, Schlatter reports that he learned from him what "a normal thought process" is.[12] The major disagreement that he registers with Beck was Beck's conviction that the modern fascination with history was misguided and damaging to the study of faith. He also studied with the early church historian, Weizsäcker, and with Overbeck. Overbeck, much like Nietzsche, impressed him as a man of great learning whose knowledge was rendered fruitless by the alienation and pessimism of his spirit.

In his theological studies Schlatter found himself more fascinated with the historians than with the dogmaticians. He reports that through his studies his thought processes became forever tied up with historical happenings. Faith, he came to see, is received through history and the scriptures. In as much as we are linked to that concrete history in faith and obedience, the history of the past creates new life and history in our experience. History is not merely something to know as a series of facts; rather it is a power that "generates new life."[13] Contra Beck, Schlatter came to the conviction that it is history that links us to God, and the modern development of historical awareness is a positive gain for the faith.

> God is creative of history, and in that through history he brings forth concrete, determinative life, the fullness of his grace is revealed. Only in this way do we have a God who is truly our God. [14]

In 1875 Schlatter became a pastor in the town of Kilchberg on the Zurich Sea. After a few months he was called to a position at the Neumünster in Zurich. Zurich at the time was in a conflict between the liberal pastors of the "reform", and the more conservative pietist pastors. Schlatter was called to be the associate of a liberal pastor. Though he reports criticism from his family and from others who resisted any criticism of orthodox dogmas, he was able to have a good working relationship with the dominant group of "reform" pastors. After a little more than a year in Zurich he was called to a small village on the Bodensee. It was there that he met his wife and was married in January, 1878.[15]

Schlatter was invited to be a candidate with the theological faculty at Berne in 1880. He was called at the behest of a conservative Old Testament scholar who felt his work among the liberal faculty could not succeed without a colleague in New Testament. At Berne Schlatter encountered a conflict that was to characterize much of his career. On the one hand he was looked to with hope by "bible believers" who associated their devotion to scriptures with a doctrine of inerrancy, and who in the name of inerrancy felt it necessary to reject scientific historical study of scripture. And on the other hand, the faculty was dominated by liberals who knew that the inerrant bible of the conservatives was "a phantom", and who held Schlatter suspect because of his "biblicism". Schlatter reports that he found himself suspect to both groups because he was neither "an uncritical biblicist" nor "an unbelieving critic."[16] Schlatter wrote his *Habilitation* on John the Baptist. Though it was accepted by the faculty, he reports that he was also informed by the Minister of Education and Cultural Affairs, that though he was now a *Privat Dozent*, he could never expect to become a Professor because the pietists would see that as a victory, a satisfaction he was loathe to give them.[17]

Schlatter taught at Berne until 1888. During this time he carried out a major research and writing project in response to a challenge from the Haager Association for the Defense of Christendom for someone to write a book on "faith in the New Testament". The jury committee accepted Schlatter's manuscript and it was released in 1885 under the title, *Der Glaube im Neuen Testament*.[18] Schlatter reports that his motive for the book was to clarify faith by showing how it arises in history. He sets himself both against the traditional idea that faith is a system of dogmas established by church or biblical authority, and the liberal idea that "religion" is a timeless reality that we may see and learn from Jesus but is not concretely rooted in the work of Jesus. In describing the method of his work in his book on faith, Schlatter describes his understanding of all his historical work:

> My logic rested on the proposition that thought history (*Denkgeschichte*) is a piece with life history (*Lebensgeschichte*), and that the life-act (*Lebensakt*) grounds the thought-act (*Denkakt*).[19]

He felt that his mission was to clarify the inner workings of how the work of Jesus gives rise to faith within the "life history" of the believer. The "thought act" of faith must be shown to arise out of the "life history" of Jesus, and must be concretely planted in the "life history" of the believer. Only then is faith rescued from being a formal, external intellectual belief so that it can become the historical means of linking our lives in reconciliation and fellowship with God.

Schlatter took up a new teaching position in Greifswald in August 1888. An interesting anecdote comes from an interview Schlatter had with a government official with responsibility for the theological faculties. The story is that the official asked if Schlatter "stood on the scriptures". His reported response; "I stand under the scriptures." Schlatter himself reports that he cannot remember what he said, but that the alleged response is true to his thought.[20] To Schlatter the government official's phrase reveals the fallacy that unites both rationalist dogmaticians and critical historians; a will to dominate the message of scripture.

At Greifswald Schlatter began a very fruitful relationship with the Lutheran theologian, Hermann Cremer. He found in Cremer a theologian whose work was to clarify and promote faith alone. Schlatter became his ally in their common opposition to the Ritschlian theology and pastors who were seeking to dominate the local church scene. Schlatter felt his opposition, however, went beyond Cremer's. While Cremer opposed Ritschlianism because it re-interpreted what was at the heart of Lutheranism, Schlatter says he went on to criticize it as well for the fact that it retained all that was *distorted* in Lutheranism.[21]

During his time at Greifswald, Schlatter began in earnest to pursue his interest in the study of Judaism. He traveled to Palestine to study geography, and especially pursued his interest in the study of the language of Pharisaism and the synagogue. His linguistic studies of Judaism laid much of the foundation for his subsequent monographs on Jewish history, and are the basis for his commentaries on the New Testament.

In 1893, Schlatter was called to Berlin University as the result of a confessional conflict within the Prussian church. The Prussian civil service had been mandated by royal decree to find a theologian who would uphold the confession and polity of the state church. Schlatter resisted the invitation pleading that he was not concerned with confessions and polity but with the scriptures and Jesus alone. The Prussian authorities persisted in their invitation, and after a time Schlatter relented.[22]

While he had lectured on both New Testament and systematics at Greifswald, at Berlin New Testament lectures were offered by Johannes Weiss who refused to have Schlatter lecturing in the same field. Schlatter's lectures were largely in the field of Systematic Theology and Ethics. Schlatter reports he had a good relationship with Harnack. He appreciated Harnack's efforts to uncover and eliminate the hellenistic heritage in Christian theology, though Schlatter felt his critical efforts had not led him back to history and the scriptures. Harnack's interest in a timeless "essence" of Christianity demonstrated to Schlatter that he had not really succeeded in freeing himself from hellenism.

Schlatter found a new outlet for his energies and ideas in 1896 when in a discussion with a group of students at Eisenach, they came up with the idea of founding a new theological journal. Schlatter took the idea to his old colleague, Cremer, and together they became the editors of the new journal, *Beiträge zur Förderung christlicher Theologie*.[23] Schlatter envisioned the journal as an outlet for any theological scholarship that was motivated by the interest of promoting the understanding of scripture and the Christian faith. He saw the journal as an organ for the promotion of historical and theological scholarship which did not conform to the assumptions and methods of the "History of Religions" approach to scholarship. Schlatter described the opposition as:

> ...the purportedly neutral, though in reality constantly polemical "Science of Religion" that seeks to overthrow Christianity by demonstrating how it came to be through the network of physical and historical causality.[24]

Schlatter's move to Tübingen came in 1898 as the result of a petition from church leaders to the Württemberg government asking that they take into consideration the interests of the church in their appointment of a professor. Schlatter accepted on the condition that he be named "Professor of New Testament" and that he be allowed to lecture on dogmatics as well. At that point in Tübingen the New Testament had been taught both by dogmaticians and by church historians. One could say that Schlatter by his insistence on his new title was carving out a new discipline that was neither simply the study of the historical origins of the church, nor the study of the church's doctrines.

It is in his Tübingen years that Schlatter produced the bulk of his writings. He notes that especially after the sudden death of his wife on July 9, 1907, he poured himself wholly into the work of writing. It would be pointless to summarize the prodigious writing production of his later years. He wrote dozens of essays on historical, theological and churchly matters. He wrote a two-part theology of the New Testament, a systematic theology, and a systematic ethic, nine major commentaries, and a multi-volume popular commentary covering the entire New Testament. He was also active in church work; conducting confirmation classes, lecturing at retreats and to groups of pastors and mission leaders, conducting bible studies with student groups and preaching regularly at the Stiftskirche in the center of the old city in Tübingen. He continued to write and speak long after his formal retirement from teaching. Dissatisfied with the methods of his replacement at Tübingen, he continued to offer seminars until the unexpected death of his replacement brought Gerhard Kittel to his old position. He held his last seminar in 1930; he died on May 19, 1938.

Schlatter's Influence

Schlatter must be regarded as a major theological factor in the German speaking world around the turn of the century. Perhaps his major influence was among pastors who looked to his writings and commentaries for a means of clear access to the message of the New Testament. His commentaries do not require the reader to work through an elaborate technical apparatus. His commentary takes one directly to the text and the theological subject matter of the faith. But apart from this more "practical" influence, I would also like to suggest four major lines of theological influence that flow from his work.

The first can easily by summarized merely by noting that the first volume of Kittel's massive *Theologisches Wörterbuch zum Neuen Testament*, is dedicated to none other than Adolf Schlatter. This is not due only to the fact that in 1933 when Kittel's first volume was released Schlatter was the grand old man of German New Testament scholarship. Schlatter was truly a pioneer in the study of the theological terminology of the Inter-testamental and the New Testament period, and of theological lexicography as a discipline. He was a major contributor to a biblical lexicon published in 1924,[25] and did extensive lexicographical work in preparation for his major commentaries, especially the one on the Gospel of John. Schlatter helped New Testament studies firmly establish that the New Testament, including the Gospel of John, can be understood only out of the linguistic heritage of Judaism—an idea that was not well received in an era when critical scholarship was "discovering" Hellenistic and Persian "parallels" to New Testament language.

Closely related to the first line of influence is the second: Schlatter as a "biblical theologian". Biblical theology as a historical discipline of course antedates Schlatter by a couple of centuries. But the early history of the discipline was fairly heavily burdened by rationalist assumptions about the "enduring message" of scripture, or by Hegelian assumptions about the dialectical logic of the historical development of religion. Schlatter represents one of the major early 20th century attempts to do a comprehensive theology of the New Testament using categories of interpretation that are reasonably true to the thought world of the New Testament itself. The biblical theology movement of the first half of this century has been both productive and plagued by a lack of methodological consensus. One of the problems over which it has stumbled is its intention to make biblical theology a descriptive historical discipline, and yet at the same time use the historian's tool box to talk about supposed "acts of God". It is interesting at least to note that Schlatter, while maintaining the distinctiveness of biblical theology from dogmatics, nevertheless rejected the idea the historical study of scripture could ever be merely descriptive, and explicitly dealt with how it is possible for the historian to deal with the question of the activity of God in history.

In this country Schlatter's influence upon biblical theology was mediated primarily through the work of Otto Piper. Several of Piper's students have mentioned how often and with what reverence he had referred to the influence of Schlatter, his former teacher.

A third line of influence is less definite and harder to trace, yet needs to be drawn out and explored: that is Schlatter as a forerunner of Neo-orthodoxy. On a superficial level the influence is evident in the fact that Schlatter was known to Brunner, Barth and Bonhoeffer, and is quoted by them. More importantly, Schlatter represents one of the few late 19th and early 20th century attempts to construct a bible-based theology that is not founded on the formal, inerrant authority of scripture or on the formal authority of a church confession. Schlatter can be seen as related to Neo-orthodoxy in his use of personalistic and historical concepts of truth and revelation, and in his attempt to replace heteronomous and autonomous models of authority with a specifically grace-oriented and personalistic understanding. Schlatter also anticipates Neo-orthodoxy's theo-centric critique of Liberal theology and the presumptuousness and barrenness of much of contemporary historical criticism.

Schlatter himself had some exposure to at least Bonhoeffer and Barth and most of his comments are quite critical. In a review of Barth's *Römerbrief*, the aged Schlatter clearly expresses the fact that he is not amused by young Barth imposing his dialectical program on the letter to the Romans. Schlatter says in effect, its nice that this young man wants to talk about God, but he has completely misunderstood Paul's letter to the Romans because he has denied any role for historical scholarship in theology, and his incomprehensible God of the dialectical "No" is not the gracious, creative God of the New Testament.[26]

Schlatter also had a chance to respond to Bonhoeffer's theology—a response that has never been published and exists only in a hand-written manuscript. In 1933, in response to the rise to power of "the German

Christians", Bonhoeffer authored the *Bethel Bekenntnis*, a formal confessional denunciation of the German Christian's theological program.
Bonhoeffer sent a copy of this proposed confession to several leading
German theologians, including Barth and Schlatter, inviting them to make
comments in the wide right-hand margins. Schlatter responded with detailed
hand-written notes and suggested emendations to the text. In brief his
criticisms were that a renewed formal confession was not what the church
needed at this time, and that Bonhoeffer's dialectical theology exalted Christ
by denigrating nature.[27]

A fourth line of influence could be associated with the "new quest"
for the historical Jesus associated with the work of Ernst Käsemann and
others. The "new quest", while fully assimilating Bultmann's insight into the
role of the church in the formation of the Gospel accounts of Jesus,
nevertheless reasserted and established a material continuity between Jesus
and the kerygma, and between Jesus and Paul. "New quest" scholarship
largely conceded that questions like the messianic consciousness of Jesus
could never be clearly answered, and rejected the idea of a biography of
Jesus. Nevertheless, it did seek to identify the distinctive ministry of the pre-
kerygma Jesus and show the lines of continuity from Jesus' career to the
early church's proclamation and theology. The "new quest" did not so much
seek to reconstruct Jesus' self-concept or a catalog of his teachings, rather
it looked at his distinctive words and actions and found in them an enacted
messianic *claim* that is picked up and made explicit in the kerygma.

Against Bultmann then, the "new quest" scholars established that
Jesus was not first acclaimed as Christ in the kerygma, but that an at least
implicit messianic claim is evident prior to Easter. Schlatter's work had
already established strong lines of continuity between the messianic claim
embodied in Jesus' acts and the messianic theologies of the early church.
Ernst Käsemann has often expressed a life-long fascination with Schlatter's
work, and I believe further study would show that he drew heavily on
Schlatter's program in his own renewed quest for the historical Jesus.

In concluding our discussion of Schlatter's influence on theology I will simply let Käsemann raise the question of what might have been. In a discussion of the possibility of a more positive relationship between biblical studies and the church, he raises the question of:

> ...why the work of Schlatter has made such a remarkably small impact on contemporary German theology. That is a quite astonishing and at the same time absolutely undeniable fact. Thousands sat at the feet of this great teacher, at least two generations of Württemberg pastors were trained by him, the influence of his writing and lectures radiated far and wide into the whole realm of German Christendom, his theological work has, for the discriminating reader, lost nothing of its actuality and fascination. He, if anyone, seemed to be called to head the movement I have just described and to provide it with a definite shape. This simply did not happen. The fact that Schlatter is little esteemed abroad can be explained to a large extent by the idiosyncratic nature of his language. But why is it that our own students hardly read him any more and are obviously given so little encouragement to do so? Why, while there are not lacking those who value him and say that he has stimulated them on individual points, are there none who have resolutely taken up and carried on his work? Why, in the very place in which his memory is kept green, is he numbered among the ranks of the merely edifying writers of typically conservative theologians in which he, one of the most valiant and liberated spirits of his generation, emphatically does not belong?[28]

Preview of the Structure of this Study

The study of Schlatter's theology is a complex undertaking. His work is comprehensive, both in the range of topics that he addresses, and in the sense that he had an eye for the relationship between the details of biblical study and the larger issues of theological method and epistemology. One cannot really isolate any part of Schlatter's work and explain it without branching out into the whole. His work must be seen as a whole, and yet we can only proceed if we isolate topics and move through them in some kind of orderly progression. This means the earlier chapters of this work will inevitably raise issues and questions that will need to be deferred until they can be taken up in detail in a later chapter of the study.

Chapter II will describe the general question of theological method as Schlatter encountered it in his historical millieu. It will show that the question of theological method, and in particular the question of faith and history is a primary motive behind much of Schlatter's work. We will also formulate a preliminary statement of this thesis of the study.

Chapters III and IV will survey Schlatter the interpreter of the New Testament. Chapter III will look at how he defined and pursued New Testament Theology as a historical discipline, and Chapter IV will look more specifically at his portrayal of "the life-act" of the Christ as it is portrayed in the New Testament.

These chapters will have raised general epistemological and methodological issues that we will then isolate and deal with in depth throughout the remainder of the study. Chapter V takes up Schlatter's original and detailed criticism of the rationalistic historical methodologies of his era. We will explain his conviction that all rationalisms which divorce truth from history are in fact "Godless" and alienate us from the possibility of understanding God's truth as it is revealed in history. Chapter VI will state his own positive philosophy of history and historical understanding. Chapter VII addresses Schlatter's anthropology and shows the critical role it plays in the integration of faith and history. To him the understanding of humankind as "personal life" created by God and meant for fulfillment in relationship to God, is a linking factor which makes it possible to see and approriate God's creative work through the "life act" of the Christ. Chapter VIII will conclude the study with a full statement of our thesis, and that is that Schlatter's understanding of God's creative grace is the ultimate integration point for his entire methodological program.

Endnotes

1.Rudolf Bultmann summarizes the history of New Testament theology as a discipline in an Epilogue to the second volume of his, *Theology of the New Testament* (NY: Charles Scribner's Sons, 1951). On pp. 248–251, Bultmann speaks positively of Schlatter's idea that the New Testament is addressed primarily to our wills, and that it views thought and action as inseparable. He agrees with Schlatter that the New Testament cannot be comprehended by the detached observer, but only by the engaged believer. What he sees as inadequate in Schlatter is his failure to realize that the historical Jesus is only proclaimed as Messiah in the kerygma. That is, Schlatter fails to see the discontinuity between "the message of Jesus" and the kerygmatic proclamation which constitutes the core of New Testament theology itself.

In personal conversation with Prof. Peter Stuhlmacher he mentioned to me that Bultmann often stated to his students that it was Schlatter who prior to him had most adequately conceived of the discipline of New Testament theology. Of course Bultmann would insist that the interpretation of the New Testament would need to be carried out now under the conditions of "demythologization".

2.Ernst Käsemann, *Essays in New Testament Studies*. (Philadelphia: Fortress Press, 1969) 4–5, 14, 84, 160.

3.Peter Stuhlmacher, *Historical Criticism and Theological Interpretation of Scripture*. trans. Roy Harrisville (Philadelphia: Fortress Press, 1977). For Stuhlmacher's discussion of Schlatter see pp. 46–68 and 70–71.

4.*Rückblick auf meine Lebensarbeit*. (Stuttgart: Calwer Verlag, 2nd ed., 1977), 19.

5.Ibid., 21–26.

6.*Die Religionswissenschaft der Gegenwart im Selbstdarstellungen*, ed. Erich Stange (Leipzig:1925), 149. This book is a collection of essays written by major historians of religion in the early 20th century. Schlatter's presentation is found on pp. 145–171. Schlatter also addresses the importance of his Reformation critique for New Testament scholarship and Christian ethics in pp. 165–169 of this essay. I address Schlatter's critique of the Reformation and its role in his theology on pp. 155–157 of Ch. VIII.

7.Ibid., 166.

8.Ibid., 165.

9.*Rückblick auf meine Lebensarbeit*, 36–37.

10.Ibid., 39.

11.Ibid., 41.

12.Ibid., 43.

13.Ibid., 49.

14.Ibid., 52.

15.Ibid., 69.

16.Ibid., 80.

17.Ibid., 89.

18.Ibid., 101.

19.*Erlebtes*, (Furche Verlag, 1924), 59.

20.Ibid., 70.

21.*Rückblick*, 141–142. The list of Lutheranism's distortions includes; "an egotistical use of faith for the interests of the self, a suspicion toward God-offered love and its work, the disdain for nature, the flight from community which is perceived only as a burden, clericalism, ...supporting the church through the power of the State, the establishment of a scholastic and authoritarian orthodoxy; all of these were not only retained by Ritschl, but continued and developed even further."

22.Ibid., 159–166.

23.Ibid., 169–174. In the early years of the *Beiträge* Schlatter published several major articles in its pages.

24.Ibid., 171.

25.*Calwer Bibellexicon* (Stuttgart:Calwer Verlag, 1924).

26.Schlatter's review of Barth's *Römerbrief* can be found in, *The Beginnings of Dialectical Theology*, ed. James Robinson. (Richmond: John Knox Press, 1968).

27.I came into possession of a photocopy of Schlatter's handwritten comments through the late Dr. Hans Stroh of Reutlingen, Germany. With Dr. Stroh's generous assistance I was able to transcribe Schlatter's archaic script handwriting into typescript.

28.Ernst Käsemann, *New Testament Questions of Today*. trans. by W.J. Montague (Philadelphia: Fortress Press, 1969), 4–5.

Chapter II

SCHLATTER AND THE QUESTION OF THEOLOGICAL METHOD

This study is essentially an examination of Adolf Schlatter's understanding of theological method. It is a fairly wide-held opinion, especially among scholars who know only Schlatter's New Testament studies or are only familiar with the milieu of piety in which his commentaries are appreciated, that Schlatter is innocent of any disciplined attention to questions of theological method. In the judgment of many of his contemporaries Schlatter was a naive intuitionist whose works were a gold-mine of practical and homiletical insights, but lacked methodological clarity and rigor and were thus of questionable scholarly value. In the words of one contemporary, Schlatter is characterized as "a religious genius and a scientific nil."[1] This widespread opinion regarding Schlatter's innocence of methodological concern has tended to consign his work to scholarly irrelevance through the label "edificational material".[2] This opinion of Schlatter is, however, a superficial conclusion which is quickly overcome when one gains some familiarity with aspects of the Schlatter corpus other than his famous New Testament commentaries.

This study will take Schlatter's two-volume New Testament Theology (*Die Geschichte des Christus* and *Die Theologie der Apostel*)[3] into consideration as resources which give us the substance of his study of the scriptures. But since we are also concerned to show how his substantive historical findings are an expression of a distinctive methodology we will also give our attention to an analysis of Schlatter's more specifically methodological writings. While this study necessitates a general summary of the results of his historical work, our more specific goal is to correlate those results with a more detailed account of various aspects of his methodology.

There are at least four different types of work in which Schlatter gives more explicit attention to issues of theological method. These four areas could be designated as: (1) explicit methodological essays, (2) writings containing analysis and critique of philosophical influences on theology, (3) autobiographical writings, and (4) his major work in dogmatic theology, *Das Christliche Dogma.*[4] The importance of the explicit methodological essays for a study of this nature is, of course, obvious. These are writings that deal critically and constructively with questions of historical method as it is applied to the study of scripture. In these essays Schlatter shows himself to be critically informed and aware of methodological issues in religious and historical epistemology and attempts to show how his biblical and theological studies are addressed precisely to those issues.

Schlatter's philosophical writings are important for this study because they show he has a keen, and even original, grasp of how the historical methods and assumptions of biblical scholarship of his day are an expression of a certain philosophical heritage. These writings also demonstrate the comprehensiveness of his epistemological interests and put to rest that idea that he is a "naive biblicist". Once one becomes aware of Schlatter's philosophical interests and insights it becomes easier to see that his work in biblical interpretation is not unrelated to his interests in formulating a comprehensive religious epistemology.

An intriguing part of Schlatter's corpus is his autobiographical reflections where we are given glimpses into the various situations of personal and professional polarization and conflict related to differing understandings of theological method which he encountered in his various teaching positions.[5] As one studies Schlatter's personal experience and his own understanding of his theological work, it becomes quite clear that he is acutely aware of the methodological concerns and crises of late 19th and early 20th century biblical studies and theology. In fact, far from being a methodological *naif*, Schlatter's entire program can be seen as a critique and an attempt to "heal" the methodological "sickness" which he believed had crippled post-Kantian biblical studies and theology.[6] Schlatter bitingly criticizes the obsession with theory of knowledge, an obsession which he believes has paralyzed and confused his contemporaries. But as he makes clear in his highly important, *Briefe über das Christliche Dogma,* the way out of the methodological conundrum of the day was not retreat into naivete or pious privatism, but even more careful attention to the subject-matter of theology, and a careful critique of unwarranted methodological assumptions that hinder access to theology's subject- matter.

Finally, *Das Christliche Dogma* is of importance to our study because it represents a crowning synthesis of Schlatter's biblical studies and his understanding of history and anthropology. In this work more than any other, the fruits of his "observation" (*Wahrnehmung*)[7] of the biblical story is brought into explicit relationship with what could be characterized as his reflective epistemological work, or even as his theologically based and reflectively developed philosophy of history.

The course of this study will bear out the contention that the methodological interest is a central question and motive that generates Schlatter's theological work, and that he deals with the question in a fairly comprehensive and sophisticated way, addressing the basic issues related to knowledge of God and theory of knowledge in general. While Schlatter is always concerned primarily with the theological interpretation of scripture, he moves freely into the realm of philosophical generalization on theory of knowledge, per se. The task that will be more difficult, and of more concern to the contemporary theologian as they consider Schlatter, is whether or not in the final analysis his work on theological method amounts to a sophisticated but defensive apology for a pious, religiously doctrinaire interpretation of scripture that is pre-given in his personal history, or if he represents a highly original synthesis of traditional Protestant faith critically combined with the insights and assumptions of modernity, especially the modern obsession with the historical question as it is applied to scripture.[8] If the latter is the case, then the originality and integrity of Schlatter's thought demands that we give him a more careful hearing than has heretofore been the case.

While the dismissal of Schlatter as naive is premature and inaccurate, there are some understandable reasons why this view arose and persists. One reason may be the character of Schlatter himself. He is a churchman who unabashedly allows his personal faith to show through in all his work. For him the distance between the lectern and the pulpit, or between faith and scientific detachment, while important, is a relative and functional distinction. Therefore, in both his exegetical and theological work he speaks both as a historian *and* a believer, *to* both the historian and the believer. So in the light of the prevailing late 19th century dogma of the complete separation between "historical" and "dogmatic" methods, Schlatter's historical work appears to be too pious or practical to be respected as science.[9] One way of stating it is to say that Schlatter sounded too pious to be a serious scholar; or to put it in another light, he did not evidence the kind of alienated consciousness which had become the mark of serious New Testament study.

A second reason behind the common opinion of Schlatter's naivete is the fact that he does not systematically establish his methodological assumptions and procedures as a prolegomena to his exegetical works. From his earliest major work, *Der Glaube im Neuen Testament* onward, Schlatter mystified his reviewers by refusing to be explicit about his methods and by refusing to carry on a scholarly dialogue with his academic peers.[10] His entire two-volume New Testament theology has two references to other scholarship! However, far from being the product of a lack of methodological awareness, he reveals in other writings which *are* devoted to discussions of method, that he consciously excluded methodological discussions from his exegesis precisely to make a methodological point.[11] He was convinced that his contemporaries had fallen into sterile treatments of the New Testament which suffered from a type of scholasticism where professional debate and maneuvering had become the primary object of New Testament studies. The result of this, in his opinion, was that the actual subject-matter of the New Testament was no longer in the historian's "field of vision" (*Sehfeld*) and that so-called New Testament theologies of the day were in fact set-pieces created for the vindication of a given scholar's methodological assumptions and procedures. This attitude is well expressed in one of Schlatter's characteristically harsh but memorable slogans, "Toward the Bible, away from the chatter of colleagues"![12]

Schlatter is unremittingly harsh in his characterization of his scholarly contemporaries, and this polarization in his own thinking and the resultant lack of scholarly exchange had the effect of making him a highly original exegete and theologian. But it also impoverished his understanding and use of critical methodologies that were emerging at the time. Nothing in Schlatter's own methodological and theological understandings would have barred him from using form or source criticism, so his lack of exchange with a wider scholarly community is indeed unfortunate. But Schlatter's analysis of the situation was such that he felt he could make the best contribution if he went his own way and as he put it, "safeguarded" his own "act of seeing".[13] His contention was that New Testament theology's task was first of all to give careful attention to what the New Testament itself had to say. Only then does the historian systematically reflect upon the question of method and how and to what extent the New Testament is understandable to us. Methodological reflection is a secondary process in which we critically retrace our path and determine how it is that we are able to understand the New Testament. The order of business for Schlatter is always *first* "observation" (*Wahrnehmung*) and *then* "judgment" (*Urteil*).[14] Schlatter felt that his post-Kantian contemporaries had reversed this order and in effect destroyed their capacity for truly open and receptive observation. As a corrective Schlatter advocated a distinct separation between the disciplines of New Testament theology where the object of one's interest is solely the subject-matter of the New Testament, and a secondary task of methodological reflection and clarification where the personal act of observing the New Testament is the object in question.[15] For clarity's sake he made a habit of dealing with these two areas in separate works. Thus his actual exegetical writings appear to be "uncritical".

Yet another reason for Schlatter's reputation is the fact that for him New Testament theology's subject-matter is solely the biblical text regarded as an expression of the "life-act" (*Lebensakt*) of the Christ.[16] The object of study is for Schlatter not the formation of the text as a literary object, nor is it the sequence of actual events that lie behind the text, nor is it the history of the ideas that are expressed in the text. All of these approaches to the study of the New Testament, in Schlatter's way of thinking, are helpful and important undertakings, but in and of themselves in a curious and subtle way they ignore the New Testament itself. Schlatter also firmly believed his own judgment that the historical events behind the biblical account and behind the formation of the text are largely hidden in darkness, and that it is not the task of the historian to illuminate obscure or forgotten historical events through conjecture. The historian's task is to observe what is there, instead of ignoring what is there (the biblical text) and seeking to reconstruct historical events through conjecture. Schlatter quoted with hearty approval J.T. Beck's dictum that, "the eyes of the wise see what is there, while the brain of the fool composes hypotheses".[17]

The biblical text itself does not present itself as a depository of events or ideas; its concern is not to communicate to us the history of its formation. Its sole concern is to present us with the claim of the Christ upon our lives. Its medium for doing this is not through ideas or simple uninterpreted objective history. The claim of the Christ is embodied or mediated through the language of the text.[18] Therefore the task of the historian in reference to the New Testament is to interpret the messianic claim of the Christ as it is expressed in the language of the biblical text. Schlatter insisted that this approach to the New Testament is, in the final analysis, more "historical" than approaches that use the biblical text primarily to reconstruct the history behind the text.

But the underlying reason that Schlatter appears naive and uncritical to his contemporaries (and to us) is that he dealt with questions of historical method and theory of knowledge as being first of all theological questions. For him historical methods were not a strictly nominal set of critical and investigative tools which the thinking subject could apply indifferently to a variety of historical objects. He set himself quite adamantly against the fairly broad consensus of his contemporaries which regarded the historian as a "neutral" scientific technician who suspended all "dogmatic" beliefs or assumptions and straightforwardly plied his historical tools in an attempt to establish *wie es eigentlich gewesen sei*. Though when it is stated that Schlatter saw questions of historical method as being primarily theological questions this does not entail that in defiance of his contemporaries he simply established a dogmatic or religiously doctrinaire view of historical method. He always rejected approaches to the scriptures which were carried out through means of a special experience of illumination or through a form of dogmatic exegesis which, in effect, denied the necessity of the historical task.

We can best begin to explain how questions of historical method are primarily theological questions for Schlatter by stating that he regarded historical understanding as a personal act. Historical investigation is not carried out by the historian as a neutral thinking subject, but is performed by the historian as a person who is necessarily determined by his personal history and interests, and who exists as a unity of thought, will and feeling. This insistence on the unity of the person, and the conviction that thought cannot be divorced from the conformation of one's will and feelings, is a central theme throughout Schlatter's work. Moreover, for Schlatter, an inescapable constituent element of personal life (*Leben*) is relatedness to God.[19] In fact it is this relatedness to God, which encompasses one's will and feelings as well as the intellect, which is ultimately determinative of all aspects of personal life, including the "thought-act" (*Denkakt*) of the scientific historian. It is this concern for the theological, or better stated, theo-relational root of methodological questions that renders Schlatter an alien to the scientific historian of his time. Schlatter's discussion of history and theological method leads always to a discussion of anthropology, and his anthropology leads always to a discussion of God. In fact, I will argue that it is his theorelational anthropology, and the understanding of God on which it is predicated which serves as his bridge between faith and history.

One of the major treatments of Schlatters's work as a whole, *Das Systematische Prinzip in der Theologie Adolf Schlatters*, by Albert Bailer, isolates "Leben" as the key to Schlatter's entire program. The thesis I am forwarding is not discontinuous with this interpretation, though I think Bailer's thesis becomes too narrow to accommodate not only Schlatter's anthropological concerns, but his concern with the object of faith as well. That is, the theme of *Leben* in and of itself is not adequate to deal with the graciously creative God who is the giver of life.[20]

This study will attempt to give a reasonably clear exposition of how Schlatter understood historical and theological work as personal acts, and how he developed a view of scientific method that is both congruent with this view of the unity of personal life and broad enough to encompass both the tasks of historical biblical theology and theological dogmatics. This exposition will lead us into Schlatter's personal and theorelational treatments of historical method, the relationship of biblical and dogmatic theology, the nature of history and historical understanding, and anthropology. But the thesis we will seek to establish is that the dynamic that underlies and ultimately determines his approach to this variety of interrelated methodological problems is his understanding of the creativity of God's grace. Both in terms of doing justice to the full range and the basic intelligibility and integrity of Schlatter as a historical figure, and in terms of making his contribution fully accessible to contemporary theologians, his work must be presented in such a manner that his understanding of the creativity of God's grace is displayed as the internal dynamic that gives form and unity to his treatment of the variety of interrelated concerns that constitute the question of faith and history.

The task of presenting Schlatter's thought as a unity is made somewhat difficult by the fact that his understanding of the creative God does not function to bring external unity to his work. It is not a formal "principle" from which the remainder of his work can be deduced. Nor does it occur as an explicit "doctrine" of God which he self-consciously uses to organize a theological system. Neither does the creativity of God connote a peculiar kind of "theo-logic" into which all aspects of the theological task are finally collapsed.[21] Rather, the creativity of God functions as an internal dynamic, sometimes explicit though more often unspoken, which shapes Schlatter's thinking about various issues related to faith and history. His wide-ranging treatment of methodological issues, including the nature of the historical task, the relationship of biblical and dogmatic theology, anthropology and theory of knowledge, are not simply derived from a prior understanding of God but rather follows the logic or issues inherent in those topics as relatively independent pursuits. Indeed it is in keeping with his understanding of the creativity of God that Schlatter attempts to safeguard the integrity of the sciences which contribute positively and constructively to the theological task. Theology conceived in such a way that other academic disciplines are either negated or used in a negative merely preparatory way is a result, in Schlatter's view, of a defective understanding of God which sees God's grace as the negation of nature and human capacities for understanding. This kind of theological heteronomy cannot speak of a God who creates and fulfills human life as fully personal life made in the divine image. While Schlatter affirms the integrity and relative independence of human life and human understanding ("science"), the thing that alienates him from most of his contemporaries is his insistence that the essentially theorelational character of human understanding dare not be suppressed in the name of a *wissenschaftlich* approach. Science that takes as an essential prejudgment that it must of methodological necessity be ignorant of God, is in Schlatter's thinking not science, but a dogmatic program in which the goal of scientific work is already given in its methodological premises.[22] One question we will need to be alert to throughout our exposition of Schlatter is how he attempts to preserve the integrity of theology related sciences while keeping them open to the question of divine agency in history. But our point here is not how he preserves both the theo-relationality and the scientific integrity of theology-related sciences; rather the point is that his particular understanding of the theo-relationality of human life and scientific understanding is best characterized by our rubric of the creative God. That is, it is his understanding of the graciously creative God who gives Himself to be known by us in the person of Jesus Christ that ultimately determines and gives unity to his understanding of the theology--related sciences and serves as the integration point of his view of faith and history.

This means that our study of Schlatter cannot simply be organized as a treatment of his doctrine of God, nor can we simply exposit his understanding of theological method and find that the notion of the creative God somehow becomes visible or can be found as it were, lying on the surface of the exposition. Our approach will be first of all to develop systematically Schlatter's understanding of theological method and its implications for a theory of knowledge. As was mentioned earlier, the problem of theological method is for him essentially the problem of faith and history. The question of faith and history is, of course, multi-faceted, but can be stated as the question of how divine agency is operative in history, and how we come to perceive and comprehend that divine agency given our own historicity. This problem is compounded or sharpened by the distinctly post-Enlightenment question of how biblical scholarship can develop a consistent and precisely defined scientific historical methodology, and how that methodology is related to the question of the perception and comprehension of divine agency in history. Schlatter himself affirms the post-Enlightenment development of scholarly canons of historical judgment and sees the separation of historical biblical theology from traditional dogmatics as a real gain for scholarship and for Christian theology.[23] His intent throughout his discussions of theological method is: 1) to critique rationalistic or doctrinaire approaches to theology that see history as a matter of indifference or as an obstacle to the theological task, 2) to critique all theories of knowledge and historical methodologies which suppress or ignore the question of divine agency in history, and 3) to develop a positive understanding of historical method which is rooted in the creativity of God's grace, and which can serve as method for interpreting scripture which is both scientifically true and can nurture the faith of the Christian community.

Endnotes

1.Many of Schlatter's contemporary reviewers saw him as more of a poet than a serious "scientific" historian. His insights are seen as "personal divinations" rather than as the product of a "certain method". The early reviews of Schlatter as an intuitionist are documented on pp. 20–26 in *Das systematische Prinzip in der Theologie Adolf Schlatters*, (Stuttgart: Calwer Verlag, 1968) by Albert Bailer.

2.Schlatter's work is a challenge to the assumption that "edification" and "scholarship" are almost necessarily antithetical. His work can be seen as a self-conscious attempt to overcome the epistemological and spiritual split that the distinction between "edification" and "scholarship" is based upon.

3.Schlatter's New Testament theology was first issued in 1909 by Calwer Verlag in one volume entitled, *Die Theologie des Neuen Testaments*. This volume was divided into two parts; "Das Wort Jesus" and "Die Lehre der Apostel". It was later rewritten and published in two volumes. *Die Geschichte des Christus*, was released in 1920, and *Die Theologie der Apostel*, followed in 1922. Calwer Verlag has most recently published the two-volume set in 1977.

4.*Das Christliche Dogma* (Stuttgart: Calwer Verlag, 1911). This work was modified only slightly before a second edition was published in 1923. I have used the second edition as it was republished by Calwer Verlag in 1977.

5.Schlatter wrote four autobiographical works:

"Die Entstehung der Beiträge zur Förderung christlicher Theologie und ihr Zusammenhang mit meiner theologischen Arbeit zum Beginn ihres fünfundzwangzigsten Bandes," *Beiträge* 25 (Vol. 1, 1920) 89ff.

Erlebtes (Furche Verlag, 1924).

Die Religionswissenschaft der Gegenwart im Selbstdarstellungen, ed. D. Erich Stange (Leipzig: Felix Meiner Verlag, 1925), 145–171.

Rückblick auf meine Lebensarbeit, ed. Theodor Schlatter (Stuttgart: Calwer Verlag, 1952).

Of course some care must be taken in using autobiographical reflections to interpret and analyze a scholar's work. Autobiographies are written at a reflective distance from the scholar's actual work and experience and that lends itself to the creation of useful and self-justifying rationales for what one has done. Schlatter's autobiographical writings will not serve as interpretive keys for his theological work, but will simply be used to provide us a window into how he experienced his historical situation as a teacher and scholar.

6.*Briefe über das Christliche Dogma*, (Calwer Verlag, 2nd ed., 1978) p. 10. This highly important series of methodological reflections written to an imaginary composite critic of Schlatter's *Das Christliche Dogma*, was first printed in *Beiträge* 16 (Vol. 1, 1912), 85ff.

7.*"Wahrnehmung"* is the key word Schlatter uses to describe his historical methodology. An English translation of this term which would adequately convey Schlatter's meaning has eluded me. The word literally means "true taking". The normal translation, "observation" seems too passive and empirical. Perhaps a better translation would be "to pay attention"; but I fear the use of such a phrase might become rather tedious. A more active, personal word like "appropriation" goes too far in conveying the idea of inward assent to that which is studied. I have chosen to use the common translation "observation". The reader will simply have to bear in mind that Schlatter is defining the meaning of this term in his own way. Note especially that to observe does not merely mean empirical noting of physical phenomena. Schlatter also pays close attention to inner events and connections.

8.Schlatter's essential modernity is betrayed in the fact that for him the question of theological method is essentially the question of faith and history. His writings contain an ongoing sharp polemic against rationalism in theology and he regards New Testament studies and dogmatic theology as thoroughly historicized disciplines.

9.It is interesting to note in this regard that while Schlatter was regarded as unscientific by many of his contemporaries, Schlatter himself could join Adolf Harnack in his attack on Barth's *Römerbrief* as "unscientific".

10.*Rückblick auf meine Lebensarbeit*, 115–116. The reasons for Schlatter's lack of dialogue with his scholarly contemporaries is detailed in Albert Bailer's, *Das systematische Prinzip in der Theologie Adolf Schlatters*, pp. 14–16.

11."The Theology of the New Testament and Dogmatics", from *The Nature of New Testament Theology*, ed. and trans. Robert Morgan. (Studies in Biblical Theology II,25) 122.

12.*Erlebtes*, 71.

13.*Rückblick*, 116.

14."Die Bedeutung der Methode für die theologische Arbeit", *Theologischer Literaturbericht*, 1908, No. 1, 6–7.

15.*Rückblick*, 117.

16.We will address Schlatter's concept of "Lebensakt" in ch. IV, esp. pp. 53f.

17."J.T. Becks theologische Arbeit", *Beiträge* 4, 1904, 32.

18.Schlatter places great stress on language as the medium which embodies and carries on the living effects of historical events. For further discussion see Ch. VI, esp. pp. 117f.

19.The term *Leben*, which I generally render as "personal life" plays a critical role in Schlatter's thought. His thought can be characterized as personalistic, though not individualistic or subjectivistic. Schlatter always dealt with the personal in relation to nature and culture. In fact he regarded Buber's popular "I-Thou", "I-It" categories as another form of dualism.

Schlatter's theological anthropology permeates his work and is explicitly developed in his *Das Christliche Dogma*, Part I, and in his major essay entitled *Die Gründe der christlichen Gewißheit* (Stuttgart: Calwer Verlag, 1917). For a treatment of the theme and how it functions in his thought see ch. VII.

20.*Das Systematische Prinzip in der Theologie Adolf Schlatters*. (Stuttgart: Calwer Verlag, 1968), by Albert Bailer.

21.Schlatter often makes the point that theology must be vindicated by thinking normally, by not making any special appeals to forms of thought or logic that are unique to theological subject matter. As he states it in *Das Christliche Dogma*, p. 558, ftn. 15, "The theologian demonstrates the correctness of his thought through the fact that he makes no claim to a special logic. Rather he thinks with the same logical rules that everyone uses."

22.For example see his, "The Theology of the New Testament and Dogmatics", 121.

23."The Theology of the New Testament and Dogmatics", 114.

Chapter III

NEW TESTAMENT THEOLOGY AS A HISTORICAL DISCIPLINE

Adolf Schlatter is justly known first and foremost as one of the great New Testament interpreters of the early 20th century. His productivity in this field is astounding. His first major academic work, *Der Glaube im Neuen Testament*, published in 1885, is referred to by Bultmann as a New Testament theology *"in nuce"*.[1]

Schlatter himself saw his commentaries on several books of the New Testament as his finest achievement, especially his influential commentary on Romans, *Die Gerechtigkeit Gottes*.[2] In addition his *Theologie des Neuen Testaments*, issued for the first time in 1909, is one of the monuments in the development of New Testament theology as a discipline.[3]

Schlatter's major academic works in the field of New Testament theology were supplemented by a long list of shorter essays and popular works. He also wrote a popular homiletical commentary on the New Testament entitled, *Erläuterungen zum Neuen Testament*.[4] I am told that this work is still one of the standard working tools of many German pastors.

A survey of Schlatter's work in New Testament theology is a rather daunting challenge. Obviously in a study such as this, which is interested primarily in theological method, a body of materials of the size and scope of his work cannot be even sketchily summarized. Apart from the sheer size of his work in New Testament, the further complicating factor in summarizing his method for New Testament studies is the nature of the methods themselves. If defining the nature of New Testament theology means abstractly stating the methods and self-understanding of an academic discipline then we are somewhat at a loss in dealing with Schlatter. His work deals first of all with concrete, material questions of biblical interpretation. Schlatter advocated and practiced a direct approach to the subject-- matter of the New Testament. It may sound rather naive or simplistic, but Schlatter's avowed method is to simply go directly to the subject-matter and see what is there. Discussions of method are secondary and reflective, and serve to clarify and defend the validity of his substantive work in biblical interpretation. One might say Schlatter is much more interested in telling us what the New Testament says than he is in convincing us that his methodology is the latest and greatest way to go about things.

Our approach in this chapter will be to first of all attempt to summarize Schlatter's more reflective formal methodological statements on the nature of New Testament theology. Then in Chapter III we will present some of the substantive issues in New Testament theology that he is concerned with throughout his work.[5] For Schlatter, New Testament theology is clearly a historical discipline. He rejects completely an older method of theology which used the scriptures as an ahistorical depository of theological doctrines. He regards the development of historical awareness and methodologies as a gain for honest scholarship. In his adoption of historical methods he is in agreement with the predominant trends in biblical studies in the late 19th and early 20th centuries.

The task of a historical study of the New Testament must also be at least initially separated from the task of dogmatics. The bible scholar must be concerned first of all with the integrity and freedom of the New Testament itself as an object of historical inquiry. The New Testament is not somehow a religious object which for that reason must be removed from the realm of historical scholarship. Nor does the historian need a special approach, or a special inner illumination in order to understand the scriptures correctly. Historical study of the New Testament follows the same rules and methods that are applied to any other object of study. Schlatter can even argue that in at least a certain sense, historical study of the New Testament follows the same rules that are applied to the natural sciences (though at other times he makes it clear that history cannot be studied in precisely the same way the natural sciences are).[6]

The Nature of New Testament Theology as expressed in "Der Glaube im Neuen Testament"

Schlatter first gives explicit attention to the task of New Testament theology in the introduction to his 1885 work, *Der Glaube im Neuen Testament*.[7] These brief statements are very significant for the understanding of this particular book and also give clear indication that from his earliest productive work he was informed, and to a certain extent motivated, by methodological interests. The methodological principles that are here merely suggested in a brief way will remain with Schlatter throughout his life and receive more sustained development at later points.

One significant methodological consideration that he clearly states at this early point bears directly on his study of faith. That is, in considering the actuality of 'faith' in the New Testament our attention cannot simply be directed toward the psychological experience of faith in the subjectivity of the believer, nor can it be directed toward faith as a formal concept whose intellectual logic can be precisely explicated. Faith certainly has both psychological and intellectual components, yet neither a psychological or intellectual explication of faith can be complete. The reason for this is that neither approach can in itself deal with the person, or more precisely stated, neither of them can address faith's relationship to the person's will. In reference to a psychological analysis of faith Schlatter writes, "Our psychological analysis (of faith), especially when it touches on realities that belong to the sphere of the will, should be undertaken only briefly at the end of the analysis."[8] The implication is that an analysis of the believer's subjectivity per se is helpful, but is not of the essence in understanding faith. This only hints at a theme that runs throughout this book and all of his biblical studies, and that is that good historical study of the New Testament will not focus primarily on the experience or subjectivity of the believer.

He applies this same principle throughout his study of faith by arguing that neither the experience of the resurrection, nor the distinctive teachings of the various apostles can be historically described or explained by reference to human subjectivity.[9] Obviously faith has a subjective component or effect which Schlatter certainly takes into constant consideration. Faith takes place in history, and for Schlatter that entails that it takes place in human subjectivity in a describable way.[10] What he has in mind in his critical remarks is an approach to biblical studies which rejects a simple historical or doctrinal objectivity in matters of faith, and then bases "religion" on "feeling". This approach to the New Testament sees in the resurrection only the achievement of a new level of religious awareness. Schlatter describes and criticizes this approach as follows:

> With these experiences [of the resurrection] there begins a new epoch in "religion". Religion is no longer faith but is characterized by the arousing of a change of feelings through which the "I" finds a new peace within itself. But we can only insert such an interpretation on our own authority because the historical sources simply will not support such a reading.[11]

For Schlatter the biblical witness and even the subjectivity of the disciples make it abundantly clear that the experience of the resurrection is not grounded in, nor does it have as its object, the religious feelings of the disciples. For one thing, the resurrection accounts are generally characterized by simple and generally calm description rather than by emotional or ecstatic fervor.[12] And above all the disciples do not describe something which originates in their own experience. Rather they describe something which they receive solely from the presence of the risen Jesus who imparts to them a possibility which is not present or even latent within their own subjectivity. So if we are going to describe historically what happened in the Easter appearances, we cannot introduce a merely subjective interpretation; if such an interpretation is to be employed it can only be introduced as an act of speculation or as a dogma.

If Schlatter has shown himself hostile to an exclusively subjective approach to faith, he expresses himself just as forthrightly on a merely conceptual approach to faith. He launches the same kind of criticism against:

...an abstract faith concept which is separated from the trusting relation-ship which is its center-point, and which gives faith its concreteness, and its power and effectiveness, but is now overlooked in the investigation. The real efficacy of faith arises from that to which the self in trust opens itself, and not to the formal course of the believer's intellectual processes. The power of faith cannot be uncovered in a faith concept which has become an empty formal concept the internal logical connections of which we need only to explicate. This abstracts faith from the reality from which the believing relationship is drawn.[13]

Schlatter rejects these approaches to the New Testament, not simply because of his prior dogmatic stance or his own personal faith (though he would not deny that these are a factor), but primarily because they are not accurate descriptions of New Testament realities. His intent is to study what the New Testament calls faith:

If we direct our investigation toward what the New Testament calls faith, it will not occupy itself with an empty, abstract faith concept. Rather it will encounter concrete faith realities (*Glaubensbethätigung*), through which faith in its fullness with its object and ground as well as with its effects can be perceived by us (*zur Wahrnehmung gelangen kann*).[14]

The inadequacy of these approaches then, is an inadequacy in historical method. Schlatter's own historical investigations are primarily of a linguistic-historical nature (as opposed to a quest for "objective history" or a study of the formation of biblical texts).[15] Therefore, the meaning of the word faith can only be made clear through an investigation of the historical relationships from which it emerged and in which it has its potency. The idea of faith is itself an empty abstraction, until it is filled in with relational content. This entails, for example, that the New Testament's understanding of faith must be understood in relationship to the synagogue. Schlatter asserts already in 1885, that a strong theological relationship exists between synagogue and church. As he states it in the introduction to his book on faith, "Not a single New Testament concept is without its precedent in the synagogue."[16] The relational character of faith also entails that the historian must not only pay attention to what the disciples believe, but must note how faith forms the will. The content of faith cannot be abstracted from obedience and the community of faith to which it gives rise. Therefore in studying faith in the New Testament we cannot only be attentive to the theology of Jesus or of the early church. We must also give attention to how Jesus on behalf of God laid claim to the believer's will, and how the believer opened him or herself in trust and obedience to Jesus as the representative of God. But the relational nature of history does not merely entail that concepts must be interpreted in light of their historical precedents, and in light of the relational aspects of faith. It also entails that a concept such as faith cannot be explicated without reference to God.

Schlatter's study of faith (indeed most of his New Testament work) is an attempt to show that faith, as it is understood in the New Testament, is the certainty of a new communion or relationship with God which is made actual through the redemptive work of Christ.[17] This certainty forms the intellect, but primarily forms the will of the believer in a new way. Through this change of will the believer is brought into a community of fellowship with and obedience to God. Therefore, if we are to give an authentic *historical* account of faith in the New Testament we must make clear the relational character of faith. And at its most fundamental level faith in the New Testament is *theo*-relational. As Schlatter states it:

> A history of New Testament concepts which is content merely statistically or chronologically to organize the material lacks understanding. The New Testament concept of faith is understood only when its basis is laid hold of, and this is found in God.[18]

A truly historical study of scripture, then, cannot ignore the question of divine causality. A methodology that seeks to understand the New Testament without reference to divine causality is fated for failure and misunderstanding. Furthermore, a methodology that begins with the assumption that the historian cannot take into consideration divine causality is not a historical method, but a dogmatic approach that holds the text in bondage to its assumptions:

> When the formation of New Testament concepts are presented only as a product of temporal, human factors; that is, when divine causality is

negated as a factor (and the ignoring of divine causality contains in it a negation); then the investigation is from the start enslaved by dogmatic premises. Negative dogmatics are still dogmatics, the only question is whether they are the right dogmatics.[19]

The historian, qua historian cannot be content with a merely neutral or descriptive account of New Testament history. The question of divine causality cannot be bracketed out of the historical task without doing violence to history itself. So our treatment of Schlatter's methodology gets us immediately entangled in substantive theological questions. Before we attempt to unravel the inter-relatedness of theological and historical methodological questions, let us take note of one other major theme in Schlatter's 1885 work on faith.

In his introduction to his study of faith, Schlatter already enunciates what will be his central epistemological principle throughout his career. He states this principle only in passing, but states it nonetheless quite succinctly, "We are not called primarily to postulate, but rather to observe what has happened". (*Wir haben überhaupt nicht zu postulieren sondern wahrzuneh-men, was geschehen ist.*)[20] A complete explanation of this principle must wait until later when Schlatter himself gives sustained attention to its significance. In this early work it, at the minimum, suggests that the historian must not import explanatory hypotheses into an explanation of the material, nor has he succeeded in explaining the material merely because a plausible hypothesis has been sustained. The historian's work is first of all pure observation of that which is given to us in the New Testament. The only thing that gives an investigation a historical character is the goal of "full objectivity".[21]

That does not mean for Schlatter that the historian is a detached observer. Far from it! While he does not clarify in this 1885 work how the interpreter's personal faith is related to historical objectivity, he does defend the idea that the personal faith of the interpreter is not a hindrance, in fact is an asset, to objectively understanding the New Testament .While the object of study is the New Testament's understanding of faith, Schlatter writes:

We should not leave unstated that the insight into the biblical view of faith which I may receive is only accessible in closest relationship to the faith which I myself have received from God's grace in Christ. It is hardly conceivable to me that without my own believing relationship, and only through my own speculation (*Phantasie*), I could penetrate and comprehend an alien spiritual environment and grasp the New Testament understanding of faith.[22]

For Schlatter the New Testament understanding of faith is so unique, and is so closely linked to the faith stance of the early Christian community, that a historian who does not identify with their view of life and does not share in the realities whereof they speak could hardly understand and interpret those realities with objectivity. The personal faith of the historian is not primarily a hindrance to objective historical study, and it most certainly should not be bracketed out of the historical task.

It is a groundless judgment to reject the serving assistance of the historian's own faith position by attacking it under the charge that it will alter the "historical character" of the investigation. Can it be that it helps rather than hinders the historian when the experiences to be studied are completely removed from anything he himself has experienced? Rather, it is in our own experience of faith in Jesus that we find the best possibility for preparing and equipping ourselves for a historically accurate understanding of the New Testament...[23]

The Nature of New Testament Theology in Later Writings

Schlatter continued to elaborate on his understanding of the nature of New Testament theology throughout his work. His reflections on the theme are scattered through a number of methodological essays, the most important of which is an essay entitled, "Die Theologie des Neuen Testaments und die Dogmatik". This essay was first released in 1909 as a companion piece to his *Theologie des Neuen Testaments*. It was published in the journal *Beiträge zur Förderung christlicher Theologie*, which was founded in 1897 by Schlatter and Hermann Cremer, and which was edited by Schlatter and Wilhelm Lütgert.[24]

As is indicated by the title, Schlatter is concerned in his 1909 essay to show the distinctions and relationship between New Testament theology and dogmatics. In chapter VII following we will look at his understanding of the nature and task of dogmatics within his entire theological program. However, we will need to give a provisional account of his understanding of dogmatics in our attempt to clarify his understanding of the historical task. Perhaps the simplest way to summarize his understanding of the two disciplines would be to say that they must be clearly distinguished, but not in a way that separates the reciprocal ties between them. Each has their own relatively independent task, yet dogmatics without history loses its content, and history without dogmatics can only show us a past to which we remain indifferent. History and dogmatics are in fact two foci, or two poles of one comprehensive theological task.[25]

The historical theological task is characterized by attention to the past:

> Our work has a historical purpose when it is not concerned with the interests which emerge from the course of our own life, but directs its attention quite deliberately away from ourselves and our own contemporary interests, back to the past. Our own convictions, which determine our thought and will, are held at a distance. We keep them out of the investigation so that we can see the subject-matter as it was. Its effect on us and the way in which it might tie in with our own thinking and willing is not at this point brought into the field of our observation.[26]

One point that needs to be noted from this quote, is that Schlatter does not posit an absolute distinction between history and dogmatics. History is not, for example, an objective scientific discipline, while dogmatics is a religious, intuitive one. The historical task is distinct and prior to dogmatics, because in it we turn our attention on what has happened in the past. But that does not quite say enough, because for Schlatter dogmatics as well are very much concerned with the past. Historical study is distinct because in it we look out beyond our own subjectivity and concerns and attempt to give rigorous attention to what happened in the past and what was once true for others. Though this particular quote may suggest it, this does not mean a naively objective approach to history. The key phrase perhaps is that the New Testament subject matter's effect on us "is not at this point brought into the field of observation".

The historian deals with the question of truth, but in a somewhat restricted way. Schlatter writes, "As historians, therefore, we can give only a partial answer to the overall question of truth."[27] This comment could easily be misconstrued. Schlatter does not mean by this that the New Testament historian should merely catalog events and concepts without passing judgment on their truthfulness. Neither does it suggest a kind of phenomenological approach which brackets out the question of truth. We have already noted that the historian must inquire after cause and effect, and cannot suppress the truth question even within the precincts of purely historical study. The historian's quest for truth is limited only in the sense that the historian is not called to say how what was once true in that time and setting remains true for us. The historian is not required to address the question of how we appropriate the past. But he or she is obligated to deal with the past in a way that does not suppress its claim to truth and authority over us. The dogmatic task differs from the historical not in that it turns away from history toward some other realm or considerations, but in that it studies history with the unrestricted question of truth. The unrestricted question of truth addresses how this past reality is an effective reality in our own experience.[28]

But in the historical disciplines the concern is only with the otherness of the past. This concern for attention to the historical otherness of the past has a dual motivation in Schlatter. First of all he believes we are created by God with an awareness of the question of truth.[29] That awareness means we cannot be satisfied with our work unless we have attempted to observe the rule of truth in our study of the past. Historical study is a response to this internal rule of truth-seeking. This rule demands that we observe the past and seek to understand its own unique claim on us before we begin to pass judgment or construct hypotheses about it. The second motivation for attention to the past is more directly theological. The task of a historical

New Testament theology is fundamental because as a believer the theologian acknowledges the scriptures as canon. Both the concern for truth and the church's theological conviction expressed as canon lead to a theological discipline in which historical study is prior to the task of dogmatics.[30]

It should be noted here then, that the status of the scriptures as canon is an essential part of a *historical* treatment of the scriptures. Just as the question of divine causality cannot be bracketed out of historical studies, so the status of the scriptures in the community of faith cannot be a matter of indifference. As has been noted, Schlatter believes the historian's personal experience and affinity with the subject-matter of the New Testament is an aid in historical understanding. This principle can be stated more broadly that the historian is part of a community of faith which regards the scriptures as canon, therefore a truly historical understanding of the scriptures cannot ignore the fact that scripture has had the historical effect of being acknowledged as canon, and that the believing historian is shaped by and is part of a community that shares that outlook. Just as the effects the New Testament message has had on the individual interpreter cannot be bracketed out of the historical task, in a broader sense the same is true of the entire Christian community. The effect that scripture as canon has had in forming a shared community of faith, cannot be wholly ignored in the historical study of the New Testament.

Once again, Schlatter makes the point in various ways, that historical study cannot be separated from personal engagement with the message of scripture. He sees the historical attitude of detachment as a product of the Enlightenment, and suggests that the idea of detached objectivity was in fact motivated by a polemical concern. Enlightenment historiography intended to separate the New Testament from the church, and thereby undermine both the New Testament and the church. But for Schlatter the ideal of detached objectivity is "an illusory fiction".[31] The nature of the New Testament message is such that it "confronts us with the claim that we should be affected by it in all our behavior and without reserve".[32] This means that while our attention is turned solely toward the past in historical investigation, and that our work must aim at "full objectivity", the dogmatic question cannot be ignored in the process. In a key statement for the understanding of Schlatter's historical methodology he writes:

> The dogmatic question may not be set aside in favor of merely historical investigation. According to the skeptical position, it is true that the historian explains; he observes the New Testament neutrally. But in reality this is to begin at once with a determined struggle against it. The word with which the New Testament confronts us intends to be believed, and so rules out once and for all any sort of neutral treatment. As soon as the historian sets aside or brackets the question of faith, he is making his concern with the New Testament and his presentation of it into a radical and total polemic against it.[33]

It is in the nature of the New Testament as an object that it makes claims. It makes the claim that Jesus is the representative of God, and it makes the claim that our lives are to be ordered by faith and obedience to Jesus as the Christ. Therefore a neutral study of the New Testament which does not allow the will to become engaged by this message is a kind of closure to the New Testament as an historical object. It effectively silences the uniqueness and historical otherness of the New Testament.

Perhaps a simple way to clarify his point here is to say that all historical work on the New Testament is motivated by personal interests. Historical objectivity consists of being clear and forthright about what your interests are, and testing those against the historical subject matter. In a rather surprising statement (considering his many criticisms of the Reformers) Schlatter suggests that modern historical criticism's assertion of its own objectivity and neutrality has been so destructive of its scientific value that many "pre-critical" interpreters have even a greater claim to scientific value! Permit me to quote at length what is a very startling quote to this effect:

> The consequence has been that those presentations of New Testament ideas which antedate the discipline of New Testament theology, such as for example Calvin's *Institutes,* have incomparably greater scientific value even as history than much of what has been done with all the tools of modern historical technique... The older writers were most seriously attentive to the relationship between what the New Testament said and the convictions by which they themselves were determined. They were

therefore resolved to clarify its contents and be certain about its truth-value. The modern historian, on the other hand, lays the ideas which determine him on one side, saying that they are his own business and not affected by his science. In fact, however, they do inevitably exercise an influence, though this is now concealed by the fiction of a merely historical purpose. They are therefore untested and ungrounded, and often enough even the historian himself is unconscious of them. With the same facility with which he passes lightly over his own convictions, he now makes judgments on the apostolic statements, too. How he interprets them and evaluates them is, of course, irrelevant for his own thought. He operates merely "historically", merely on an object which is dead and gone.[34]

So the critical historian operates on a kind of bad faith. On the most obvious level his supposed neutrality is in fact a cover for polemical interests. For Schlatter, objectivity does not mean "presuppositionless" interpretation, but an ever more rigorous attention to our presuppositions. His rule for increased objectivity is stated very well when he writes, "However, we shall only get free of and rise above our presuppositions by paying conscious and rigorous attention to them".[35] But on a more subtle level the fact that the historian is no longer *personally* interested in the New Testament and no longer regards it as intertwined with his or her life and therefore of vital interest weakens the motivation to observe the rule of *truth* in historical work. Pre-critical interpreters had a more vital personal interest in scripture and so had more at stake in clarifying the content and the truth-value of the New Testament message. Schlatter of course realizes the danger of scriptural truth being subordinated to dogma; in fact it is a major theme of his work. But his more original insight here is that a claim to neutral disinterested objectivity can result in a lack of care and concern for the question of truth since the results of such a study are supposedly of no personal concern to the historian. Since the results of a "neutral scientific" study of the New Testament are supposedly of no personal interest to the historian any kind of fantastic conjectural explanation becomes a possibility.

Schlatter sees a relationship between the historian's supposed neutrality and the failure of contemporary historian's to carefully *observe* historical realities. Just as they are unaware of what shapes and determines them as historians, they disregard what shaped and determined the apostolic witness. What is offered to us as biblical scholarship is now a series of conjectures in place of careful observation:

> Historical study of the New Testament has given way to an attempt to thoroughly reconstruct the history behind the texts and behind the formation of the text. And this reconstructive effort takes place in the imagination of the supposedly objective historian.

So while Schlatter argues that history and dogmatics are inseparable; or that our efforts in historical science cannot be separated from who we are as persons, he still advocates a distinction between the two functions. The past deserves to be studied on its own simply because it exists as something given and separate from us. Once again there is a personal, or even moral, issue involved here:

> The question here is whether we are all wrapped up in ourselves, or whether we are able to be genuinely open to the past so as to be able to see things other than ourselves.[36]

This goal is enhanced by the development of a separate discipline that asks about the content of the New Testament solely for its own sake. This priority on historical study for its own sake is both good science and consistent with faith. Since it is the church's claim that it finds the saving work of God in the message of Jesus and the apostolic witness to Jesus, the church's good conscience depends on disciplined attention to that message in and of itself. If we begin to do our study at the point of our own interests and ideas the question of truth is once again hampered:

> If we turn our attention straight away to the connections which exist between our object and our own ideas and will, then there is always a danger that we will break off our observation at the point where our own interest in the object ends.[37]

Therefore, in the interest of checking our own interests and ideas and making good on our intention to hear truly the message of the New Testament, historical disciplines play an essential role in the theological task:

The justification for a New Testament theology conceived as history is the independent development of historical science gives a measure of protection, admittedly not infallible, against arbitrary reconstructions of its object. It secures us against producing a mixture of what scripture says and what the church teaches, or a mixture of the Bible and our own religious opinions, in which neither the one factor nor the other is correctly grasped and fruitfully applied.[38]

For Schlatter, then, the historical sciences play a central, rather than a merely preparatory role in the task of theology. Faith may not enlist in its service any appeals to personal illumination or a privileged fideistic stance in order to by-pass the normal historical sciences. Schlatter's complaint is not against historical critical study, indeed historical criticism properly understood *is* his theological method. His complaint is against a historical science that has lost its objectivity and has become a form of dogmatism, and his program is to redeem New Testament theology as a discipline by recovering its proper object.

Endnotes

1.Rudolf Bultmann, Theology of the New Testament (NY: Charles Scribner's Sons, 1951) vol. II, 248.

2.For a complete list of Schlatter's major commentaries, see the heading "Major Commentaries" in my Selected Bibliography, pp. 180.

3.See endnote 3, ch. II.

4.Schlatter's *Erläuterungen zum Neuen Testament*, was first published by Calwer Verlag in 1908. It was last released in 1987. Intended as a popular commentary for "bible readers" it covered the entire New Testament in 10 volumes.

5.Schlatter spoke of New Testament theology rather than simply biblical theology. This is not because the Old Testament has no role in his theology, but because he believed that for the Christian community our "*Gemeinschaft*" with God is mediated to us through the Christ who is proclaimed in the New Testament. One can only wonder what the effect would have been on biblical theology as a discipline had Schlatter's approach been more influential. Certainly the biblical theology movement would have been less dominated by Old Testament studies.

6.See Ch. VI, p.112f.

7.See *"Einleitendes"* (Introduction) in the first edition of *Der Glaube im Neuen Testament*. This introduction to the first edition is also included in the 1977 Calwer Verlag release of the same book (see pp. XIV–XXIII). Schlatter also deals briefly with methodological issues on pp. 131f., 236f., 286f., and pp. 318–323, and in footnotes on pp. 348 and 401 (page numbers are from 1977 release).

8.*Der Glaube im Neuen Testament*, XIVf.

9.See *Der Glaube im Neuen Testament*, pp. 236f. for a discussion of subjective theories of the resurrection. We will show later that Schlatter in a sense does recognize the primacy of human consciousness, and agrees that the New Testament passes on to us the experiences of the early apostolic community. But for him subjectivity is the starting point, and our attempts to understand the New Testament must go beyond the subjective consciousness of the apostles to an examination of the object towards which their experience points and on which it is founded.

10. Ibid., XVII. Schlatter never hesitates to describe the anthropological coordinates of faith, even if faith is not reducible to anthropology. To him a faith that is not anthropologically describable (even though it is not exhaustively describable) is a destructive and therefore unbiblical faith. Faith, for Schlatter, establishes and enables personhood. He rejected Barth's dialectical theology because the "wholly other" God of Barth's, *The Epistle to the Romans*, does not enter into communion with humanity and therefore negates rather than establishes our personhood.

11.Ibid., 236.

12.Ibid., 236–237.

13.Ibid., XV.

14.Ibid., XV.

15.Ibid., XVI. For Schlatter the study of history is primarily the study of language. He did his work before many of the major resource materials in this field were available. He is a pioneer in research on the Judaism of the 1st century and its influence on the speech and thought of the New Testament. Most of his writings in this area are the result of his own extensive linguistic research. He pioneered in lexicographical studies and was a major contributor to the *Calwer Bibellexikon* edited by Hermann and published in 1924. For a discussion of Schlatter's understanding of the relationship of language and history see ch. VI, pp. 115ff.

16.Ibid., XIX.

17.Schlatter consistently states that faith is certainty (*Gewißheit*) of God's redemptive work in Christ. Certainty is not primarily an intellectual claim, but a personal one. Certainty is a category of the will and it works to form and empower the self. It plays a critical role in Schlatter's theology and methodology. He also wrote a major anthropological and theological essay on the topic, *Die Gründe der christlichen Gewißheit* (Stuttgart: Calwer Verlag, 1917).

18.*Der Glaube im Neuen Testament,* XVI–XVII.

19.Ibid., XVII.

20.Ibid., XVII.

21.Ibid., XXII.

22.Ibid., XXII.

23.Ibid., XXII.

24.This essay is one of the two major Schlatter writings that have been translated into English. It can be found in *The Nature of New Testament Theology*, edited by Robert Morgan. Schlatter himself describes the reasons for the founding of the journal and its relationship to his theological work in an article entitled, "Die Entstehung der Beiträge zur Forderung christlicher Theologie und ihr Zusammenhang mit meiner theologischen Arbeit", *Beiträge*, vol. 25, 1920.

25.See my discussion in ch. VII, p. 143–145.

26."The Theology of the New Testament and Dogmatics", 118.

27.Ibid.

28.Ibid., 119.

29. Schlatter makes much of the idea that there are certain laws or givens that our part of our God-created make-up. Among these are the sense of obligation that we have to seek truth. He develops this in his essay *Die Gründe der christlichen Gewißheit*. He discusses this rule of truth seeking and its relationship to historical study in pp. 40–51.

30. See "Theology of the New Testament and Dogmatics", p. 120, for Schlatter's discussion of the relationship of canon to the historical task. Of course the idea of canon is not only a historical judgment, but is part of the community's dogmatic convictions. For Schlatter these convictions help to motivate and shape the historical task. So since canon is a historical effect that the scriptures have had in the life of the church (and the historian who is part of that church) the judgment that scripture is canon should not be bracketed out of the historian's field of view. This again shows that historical and dogmatic issues cannot be totally isolated from each other.

31. "The Theology of the New Testament and Dogmatics", 120.

32. Ibid.

33. Ibid., 122.

34. Ibid., 124.

35. Ibid., 127.

36. Ibid., 122.

37. Ibid., 127.

38. Ibid., 128.

Chapter IV

THE GOAL OF NEW TESTAMENT THEOLOGY

Schlatter was convinced that the study of the scriptures had been grievously injured by the predominance of neo-Kantian canons of critical reason. This had come to mean that the "scientific historian" cannot seek after ultimate causes or explanations. The historian can seek to give an orderly or objective account of the sequence of historical events, or can seek to order and explain the ideas we find in Jesus or the apostles. But for Schlatter this is not a complete understanding of the historical task. Merely to order the sequence of historical events is incomplete since that does not in itself explain them. Nor does seeking out the intellectual content of the New Testament really help us understand the significance of the New Testament. Usually such accounts seek to explain the origin of these ideas in some vague theory of how "world-historical ideas" originate in the consciousness of a "religious genius".[1] But such explanations are conjecture and are not derived from rigorous attention to the New Testament itself.

The historian's task must be to explicate, in as much as is possible, a past event by relating it to its causes and its effects.[2] Events do not have a kind of self-explanatory power in and of themselves. Historical events are part of a vast complex of events, so historical understanding requires that any given event be set in relationship to the events which caused them and which they in turn cause. Only then is a historical event not only described but also understood.[3]

The New Testament mediates to us a wealth of historical information. It relates to us a series of events related to the life and ministry of
Jesus. But obviously the writers of the New Testament intend to do much
more than pass on information about those events. The New Testament also
communicates the content of Jesus' teachings and the content of the apostolic
community's teaching about Jesus. And yet as we have already noted
Schlatter contends that the significance of Jesus cannot be grasped simply
from a study of his teachings. It is also obvious that while the New
Testament contains apostolic teaching about Jesus, the understanding of the
apostolic teaching is not an end in itself. In order to comprehend it we must
ask how it arose and what function it intended to serve. So neither an
understanding of the sequence of events, nor the formal teaching content of
the New Testament itself is an adequate goal for New Testament theology.

The Life-Act of the Christ as the Object of New Testament Theology

Schlatter sees the entire New Testament as a unified whole. As he
himself expresses it, his motivation for his major works *Die Geschichte des
Christus*, and *Die Theologie der Apostel*, was that in contrast to the biblical
scholarship of his day, "The history of Jesus always presented itself to me
as a unity."[4] Biblical studies in the late 19th and early 20th centuries were
engrossed in the task of breaking the old dogmatic theological unity of the
New Testament. In its place they were finding a "historical Jesus" who in
as much as he was knowable was quite different than the apostolic
community's "Christ of faith". This "historical Jesus" was also wholly at
odds with the Jewish community and taught religious and moral concepts
that had no rootage or vital connection to his own community. Within the
apostolic tradition they were finding different "circles" which interpreted
Jesus in different and often contradictory ways. The Jesus of the Gospel of
John is quite another being than that which is found in the synoptics, and the
Jesus of Paul is still another almost independent tradition within the early
church.[5]

To Schlatter, the disintegration of the unity of the New Testament is not an inevitable result of the historical study of the New Testament, and he in no way meant to return to the dogmatic "harmonization" of the theological content of the scriptures. Rather, he saw the disintegration of the unity of the New Testament as the outcome of a historical method misunderstood and misapplied. The unity of the New Testament had been lost because historians had lost their grip on what the central goal and object of historical study of the New Testament should be. In describing his vision of the unity of the New Testament Schlatter wrote that in his study of the New Testament:

> I saw him (Jesus) before me with one calling and one goal that generated the entirety of his words and his works. And this unity did not appear as the artificial product of my attempts at harmonization which veiled the particularity of singular words and events, but rather as the outcome of the most rigorous and concrete appropriation of their actual historicity...
>
> I saw no great gap between the work of Jesus and his disciples, or between his call for Israel to repent and his founding of the Christian church, or between the work of Peter in Jerusalem and that of Paul among the Greeks. Rather I possessed one unified New Testament. And this was not because my apologetic intent and skill had devised this, but because I found a tightly bound together history that was created throughout its course by the same powers; powers that originated in Jesus and from him went on to bring forth the apostolic community and its documents. That is why alongside the many other studies of the New Testament community which presented it as torn by a thousand contradictions, I presented mine.[6]

A couple of very important points are clearly evident from this quote. The first is that Schlatter moves very freely from a discussion of the person of Jesus, or Jesus' unified sense of call, to a discussion of "a unified New Testament". That is because in his methodology those questions are one in the same. The object of study in the historical study of the New Testament *is* "the story of Jesus" (*die Geschichte Jesu*).[7] Schlatter would say that this focus on the story of Jesus as the object of any historical study of the New Testament is a clear and obvious conclusion from any serious historical observation of the New Testament—that is, his Jesus focus is not simply a dogmatic decision or a result of his personal religious sentiments.

The New Testament itself does not ask us to study the distinction between the historical Jesus and the Christ of faith; it always portrays Jesus as a unity throughout his career. Neither does the New Testament itself point us toward a study of the origin of the various apostolic communities and their personal and theological differences. Nor does it invite us to diligently inquire into the history of how the various New Testament documents came to be. Everywhere it points us toward Jesus' career. It describes his origin from God, his ministry among his fellow Jews, his death and resurrection, and how his work continued into the apostolic communities through the work of the apostles and the presence of the Holy Spirit. *This* is what the New Testament itself intends to portray to us so *this* is what the object of our study must be if we are to understand the New Testament. We are of course free to study the histories of the various communities and the formation of the biblical text, but when we do, Schlatter would say, we are not doing the primary task of the historical study of the New Testament.

Another clue that needs to be drawn from the preceding quote concerns the nature of the unity that Schlatter thought he clearly saw in the New Testament. The interesting phrase here is that in which says he found, "a tightly bound together history that was created throughout its course by the same powers;..." This suggests, and further study will bear out, that the unity he sees is of an internal and personal sort, rather than external and intellectual. Schlatter can and does concede that there is not a precise factual coherence among the four gospels as they present Jesus' life. He is also clear that the teaching of the apostles does not in itself contain a formal intellectual unity. The unity he finds (or is it the unity he seeks?) is of another order. It is that the New Testament story is a unity because it contains a discernable order that is a product of certain "powers" that shape and direct its course. And clearly for Schlatter this order and the "powers" that lie behind it is of a personal nature.[8] There is a distinctive life pattern, an order of outlook and action, that characterizes the "life-act" of Jesus. One might say that what Schlatter seeks to find in the New Testament is a

Jesus "*gestalt*" that was evident in his life and in the effect he had on those who later bore witness to him.

The concept of Jesus' "life-act" is a complex one, but vitally important for understanding Schlatter as a historian. The concept of a "life-act" is not simply a way of talking about Jesus' personality and the lively impression it made on others. A person's "life-act" encompasses their deepest motivations and how those motivations are enacted within their particular environment. It assumes that personal life is an intelligible unity of thought, will, feeling and action. Furthermore, an individual's life is only intelligible in reference to the social environment within which it is lived out. Therefore it is an unhistorical approach which regards Jesus as a religious "genius" who somehow amazingly transcends the thought and conditioning of his own community and generates hitherto unknown ideas or moral values.[9] For Schlatter idealism and individualism are corrupted ideas of what the human person is. For him the person receives the form and content of their life from history and from the community that bears that history, and in turn lives out their life in relationship to the community.

Furthermore, the idea that the historian must study and portray the "life-act" of Jesus must be correlated with what Schlatter regards as one of the givens of historical methodology—the rule of historical continuity. For Schlatter history can only be understood if the historian assumes and rigorously follows the rule of historical continuity. Thus the "life-act" of the Christ must be investigated and portrayed by the historian according to the most rigorous application of the rule that history is a continuity. If Jesus' life cannot be studied and presented under that rule then it is essentially unintelligible to us and therefore unproductive for us. Here again, Schlatter shows that in a sense he is in agreement with late 19th century historicism. If history is to be "scientific" it cannot tolerate the idea of unexplainable leaps and gaps which are bridged by abrogating normal rules of cause and effect.

The problem with post-Kantian historicism from Schlatter's perspective is not its insistence on historical continuity, but its dogma that continuity must always be explainable in immanentist terms. Clearly the New Testament means to portray Jesus in terms that transcend that and which claim that his "life-act" uniquely originates in and is oriented toward God. The "life-act" of Jesus is ultimately presented in the New Testament as the saving encounter of God with His people. The historical study of Jesus then cannot ignore that claim or exclude it from consideration a priori. Schlatter also differs from post-Kantian historicism in that his fundamental motive for affirming the continuity of history is theological. Unless the "life-act" of Jesus can be presented as an intelligible continuity which originates in God and terminates in our faith in Jesus, then Jesus cannot be the agent of a creatively gracious God who wills to recreate us in the divine image.

The New Testament claims that what is unique or distinctive about Jesus is how he comports his will and thought in relationship to God, and how that is manifest in his words and deeds in relation to Israel and the apostolic communities. To exclude that claim from the scope of historical investigation is to not really attempt to understand the New Testament. But, the historian might ask, how does one devise a methodology to study and evaluate that claim? Schlatter's answer is that one studies and evaluates it primarily by rigorous "observation" of the story itself; and in the New Testament that story is clearly from beginning to end, the story of the "life-act" of Jesus.[10]

Jesus and the Jewish Community

A major concern in Schlatter's portrayal of Jesus is to show that his career can only be understood within the context of the Jewish community of which he is a product, and to which he addresses himself. Johannes Heinrich Schmid, in a comparative study of Schlatter's and Martin Kähler's approaches to Jesus, begins his section on Schlatter by writing, "Schlatter portrays the story of the Christ as the story of the encounter of the messiah with his community."[11] Jesus is not a timeless or transcendent individual who somehow happened to carry out his work in a Jewish setting, nor does he come from outside of that setting in order to correct its ideas and practices. Schmid shows that Schlatter believed that Jesus takes the understanding of faith that he finds in his community and adds nothing new to its content. Jesus receives the givenness of his communal heritage and accepts it as the framework for his career and for his relationship with God. Jesus then was never in conflict with Jewish understandings of theology and faith. The conflict that was generated by his life arose out of the sense of "certainty" (*Gewißheit*) that governed his relationship to God and the claims and actions that arose out of it.[12] Jesus confronts God's chosen people not with new ideas about faith but with a new personal *claim* to which they must respond. Jesus carries within himself a confidence or certainty that he is empowered by God to call Israel to repentance and in the name of God to challenge and overthrow any faith that is not truly and singularly directed toward the God of Israel.

Schlatter's portrayal of the faith of Israel is contained both in monographs dedicated to that topic alone, and in his major presentations of Jesus.[13] His studies in historical linguistics of early Judaism are quite extensive and constitute in themselves a major scholarly contribution. The details of his study of Israel's faith at the time of Jesus go beyond the scope of our study, but a brief sketch will be helpful.[14] He portrays Jesus within two critical elements of the Jewish community; the Pharisaic understanding of faith and law, and the eschatological expectations of the community.

First of all it must be said that Jesus shares a great deal with the Pharisees. He shares with them the conviction that Israel's life is to be governed solely by its relationship to God. God calls Israel to an absolute trust in Him. That faith is to form and permeate all aspects of the community's life. In the pharisaic understanding there is to be no hiatus between faith and life, or between one's inner relationship to God and the acts that characterize one's outer life in relationship to others. There is to be no break or division between God's grace in electing and redeeming his people, and our response of whole-hearted trust and obedience. Devotion to God is inseparable from how that devotion is concretely manifest in life.

But Schlatter suggests that Jesus sees in Pharisaism an outlook and practice that belies their understanding of faith, and separates that which should be unified. While Jesus shares with them a conviction that God is to be obeyed in all of life and that God's will is revealed in the inspired scriptures, he finds and exposes the contradictions of Pharisaism which are driving Israel away from trust in God and whole-hearted obedience. Out of their respect for God and the demand for obedience, they had given undue respect to the interpretive work of the rabbis. The legal interpretations of the rabbis became a formal, externalized ethic of obedience to which believing Jews were called to give their trust and allegiance. In Schlatter's understanding, this produced contradictions that ultimately separated Israel from God. In as much as the law became externalized it shifted the believers focus onto him or herself. The believer's relationship came to be grounded not in the grace of God, but in how the believer's acts were determinative of how God reacted to the believer. An absolute trust in God became confused with the question of the adequacy of the believer's obedience. The result is to introduce uncertainty and alienation into the relationship. The uncertainty of human accomplishment called the relationship with God into question. God's will became formalized and external to the believer, thus not something freely appropriated into the inner life and motivations of the believer. And since the believer sought to draw near to God through an exertion of the will, God himself became remote.

Jesus' work in relation to the Pharisees, then, is to expose hypocrisy and the destructiveness that pharisaic piety brought to Israel. But more positively stated he brings with him what Israel lacked—a new sense of confidence in the nearness of God's saving presence. It is his messianic deed to live out of this new confidence and to call Israel to repentance and to receive this saving presence of God through his ministry.

Jesus also shared with Israel an expectation of future salvation. Schlatter makes a very sharp distinction between the prophetic and apocalyptic forms of eschatological expectation. Apocalyptic with its pseudonymous authors and its speculations about the future is "midrash" on the prophetic tradition, and, Schlatter believes, Jesus was clearly not influenced by it. To him Jesus represents a return to the prophetic promise and confidence that is an essential part of Israel's heritage and scriptures. Jesus does not announce a far distant complete disruption of history in which God will set everything right. Rather he lives and acts in a complete confidence in God's present act through him to establish a new community of faith and obedience which is the manifestation of God's coming salvation.

In light of his confidence in God's saving presence in the present, Jesus undertook to challenge and overthrow that which has been distorted in Israel's expectations. Schlatter sees Jesus in conflict with two basic distortions in Israel's hopes. The first is the tendency for the eschaton to be a nationalistic glorification of Israel. While eschatological hope can never be separated from the question of the destiny and glorification of Israel as the people of God, the apocalyptic tradition portrayed the coming kingdom as an uncritical establishment of Israel and its institutions. There is acknowledgement that Israel contains sinners who will be judged along with the heathen, but there is also the unbroken conviction that there is an enduring righteous Israel. The eschaton will be a vindication of these physical sons of Abraham and of their religious institutions, the temple and the law.

The second major distortion in Israel's hope is the causal link that is established in Pharisaic piety between Israel's efforts at obedience and the bringing in of the kingdom. While no Jew could doubt that it was God who would bring in the kingdom, an understanding did develop that Israel's keeping of the law could somehow control or influence God's actions. Schlatter labels both of these distortions as "irreligious" because they reject God's sole prerogative and initiative and make human institutions and actions the controlling center of God's actions.[15]

Jesus, in continuity with John the Baptist, challenges the first distortion by a demand for the absolute necessity of repentance.[16] Being a

Jew by virtue of Abrahamic descent, or being righteous as the Pharisees
define righteousness, does not qualify one for the kingdom. All of Israel is
summoned to an act of repentance. But this call for repentance also refutes
the second distortion mentioned above because it is predicated on the
absolutely gracious saving nearness of God's kingdom in Jesus. Jesus acts
with unique certainty and authority to offer in God's name that which Israel
did not expect; that the inauguration of the kingdom would bring about the
establishment of a new relationship with God. Jesus offers a new basis for
Israel's life as the people of God by announcing and enacting God's will to
forgive and renew His people by the presence of the Spirit. It is the
unprecedented and unexpected graciousness of this act which makes
repentance imperative.[17] Israel's relationship with God is no longer to be
governed by law and nationalistic hopes which ignore God's graciousness.
Instead their communal life is to be governed by faith; by an unqualified
confidence in Jesus as the messianic act of God.

Schlatter sees Jesus, not the apocalyptic tradition or Pharisees as the
true inheritor of the prophetic messianic promises, because he alone looks
to God alone for redemption, and because he alone sees the new age as
characterized by a new covenant of grace and the Spirit. It is Jesus'
messianic activity which captures the universal impulse of the prophetic and
Davidic expectations and makes it an actuality.

The Messianic Will of Jesus

Schlatter consistently makes the point that Jesus' life cannot be
comprehended apart from his encounter with the Jewish community. We
have attempted to summarize that encounter in the preceding section. Yet,
Schlatter's methodology does not stop at "observing" this public encounter
between Jesus and his community. He commonly states that the historian's
task is to observe both "inner and outer events" as parts of the whole
event.[18] Jesus' encounter with his community can be characterized as an
observable "outer" event, but Schlatter would say we cannot comprehend

his "life-act" until the "inner" events of his life are observed and understood as well. What is meant by "inner" events here is not simply Jesus' inner life or psychological make-up. The "inner events" of Jesus life are observable in his public words and deeds. "Inner" events are those motivations and relationships which characterize Jesus' will and which are given expression in his words and deeds. Jesus' career cannot be illuminated simply by summarizing his deeds or his teachings. The first and most basic task required of any attempt to comprehend the New Testament, what it means and how it came to be, is to "...make visible what Jesus carried within himself as his fundamental certainty and how everything that he did followed from that".[19]

The New Testament presents us with the words and deeds of Jesus. But the scientific task is not to figure out whether they are early or late sayings, or whether they come from Jesus or are amended by later interpreters. That kind of a study leads into speculation and conjectural reconstructions that do not lead us any closer to knowing Jesus. The words and deeds that the New Testament presents are there because they make known the will which constantly determined his outlook and actions. The scientific historical task is to penetrate the words and deeds of Jesus story in order to comprehend the will that motivates them. As Schlatter himself describes the goal of his work in New Testament theology he writes:

> In that it (the New Testament) places before us a wealth of clearly observable events it calls us to the scientific task that is actually potential- ly fruitful. Namely, it calls us to think through the many particular words and deeds of Jesus in such a way that the ground out of which they are generated is made visible to us... Therefore our view will be directed toward the inner root, not toward the visible aspect of events... [20]

For Schlatter, the "inner root" that is clearly visible in all of Jesus' words and acts is his "messianic" or "kingly" will.

Schlatter's major presentations of Jesus, for example in his *Die Geschichte des Christus* and *Das Christliche Dogma,* follow the form of sustained narration of Jesus' career and identity. The constant theme of these presentations is that Jesus career can be seen as a coherent unity only if his "messianic will" is seen as the goal and reference point that explains all his actions and words.[21] In his essay, "Der Zweifel an der Messianität Jesu", his argument is that if you take away from any part of Jesus' career the realization that all of his life was determined by his messianic calling, his life loses its coherence and unity and one ends up with "gaps" and "puzzles" that destroy historical continuity.[22] To tell the story of the Christ, then, means to describe how the king encountered his community. Messiahship is not a substance or an idea in the mind of Christ; it is an act. And as an act it cannot be abstracted from the specific, contingent event of the messiah meeting and claiming his new community. In a statement that goes far in explaining Schlatter's Christology he writes, "It is in the act that the essence makes itself visible, and in such a way that it is not essence apart from the act."[23]

For Schlatter, the messianic character of Jesus' "life-act" is not comprehensible if one begins from the point of the cross and resurrection.[24] There is no way to coherently explain how experiences or visions of the resurrection of a crucified man could have in itself awakened messianic convictions. Jesus must be understood as the messiah in his earthly life in order for the culmination of his life to be understood. Jesus did not see his mission on God's behalf to be to die, rather it was to live for God by living for Israel. The story of Jesus has no interest in explaining Jesus' own personal pilgrimage and how he came to have a messianic will. At no point in the tradition do we get a glimpse of a Jesus who had a self-understanding that was other than messianic.[25] From beginning to end of his story he is in possession of a messianic will that guides and directs his encounter with Israel. The Jesus story is a drama and all the highlights of that drama revolve around how the anointed king encounters his community, is rejected by that community, creates a new fellowship among the disciples, is crucified and raised to live on as the lord of a new community of faith and the Spirit.

Once again, we can only briefly sketch how Schlatter portrays Jesus' messianic will. Already in his call to repentance Jesus displays the nature of his messianic will. The messiah comes not merely to redeem an already completed community. His essential work is to enter into fellowship with an unredeemed community of promise and truly create it as the people of God. The kingly work of the earthly Jesus is revealed in that he comes to awaken faith and to create a new community of faith and obedience. In this call to repentance and his claim that through faith in him Israel enters into the fellowship of the kingdom of God, Jesus reveals that he possesses the certainty that he is commissioned to act on God's behalf.[26]

The kingly will of Jesus is manifest in that he does not simply speak words that are of God or that call people to God, but in the fact that he acts with divine authority and power.

> The Christ is not one who describes or teaches the lordship of God, but is the one through whom it happens. He is not the one who portrays the consummated community, but is rather the one who creates it and rules over it. Lordship occurs not through words but through power. The king shows himself as such through his work.[27]

It is clear especially from his encounters with the Pharisees that Jesus was free to announce and enact a new reign of God characterized by forgiveness and grace, and in the name of that new reign of God to call all Israel to be subordinate to him. Jesus' messianic will, though it did not have the judgmental ruling form that Israel expected, always remained messianic in that it was always a call for obedience and submission to the will of God.

It was this demand for repentance and obedience predicated on grace that the Pharisees rejected. And again, it is a manifestation of Jesus' messianic will that he broke with the Pharisees and rulers and rejected and undermined their claim to be the interpreters of the law and the rulers of Israel.[28]

Another major aspect of the messianic drama is Jesus' calling of the disciples. And in this event too, the messianic will of Jesus is manifest. In calling disciples Jesus does not turn away from Israel and the universal messianic task. The calling of the disciples is not the founding of a sect, instead it manifests Jesus' confidence that he is called and empowered to found a new community. The calling of the disciples shows that while Jesus directs his work toward Israel, he is not dependant on Israel's acceptance to authenticate his kingship. His kingship is from God and he is free to gather a disciple community from among Israel.[29]

It is important to note that for Schlatter, Jesus' calling of the twelve is not in itself the founding of the messianic community. That awaits the messiah being revealed in glory.[30] But the twelve do anticipate the new community. It is the disciples who have responded to Jesus' call to repentance. It is they whom Jesus teaches and to whom he reveals his calling. It is they who are privileged to see the glory of God displayed in Jesus' work, and it is they who confess Jesus' messianic mission. And finally it is among his disciples that Jesus anticipates his final destiny and reveals that his coming fate is not an accident, but his final act of service on the community's behalf. In calling the disciples Jesus shows already in his earthly life,..."that he has the power to forgive, to release from guilt and to create the purified community to whom he promises the baptism of the Spirit."[31]

The supreme messianic act of Jesus was the cross. As Schlatter succinctly states it, "The kingly act of Jesus was the cross."[32] Jesus came to live for God by living for Israel. His entire life was filled with salvific meaning. In his entire ministry the creative lordship of God is enacted and made effective. That means that the messianic work of Jesus cannot be reduced to his work on the cross. Nevertheless, the cross is the culmination of his encounter with Israel, and is also the decisive revelation of his messianic will.

The event of the cross grows out of Jesus' encounter with Israel and is the revelatory disclosure of the nature of his mission. The event of the cross is both "outwardly" and "inwardly" a result of his mission to Israel. "Outwardly" it is the result of the total character of his call to Israel and the radical nature of the messianic claim embodied in that call. If Jesus had, for example, only claimed to be the messiah there would not have been any utter necessity for the Pharisees to seek his death. But in that his messianic claim was a call for repentance and the offering to Israel of a new basis for its relationship to God, Israel is compelled to accept or utterly reject him. While Schlatter would say we cannot know precisely how Jesus became aware of his destiny on the cross; he seeks to show that Jesus became aware of its inevitability in light of Israel's rejection of him, and that having that awareness he positively embraced the cross as the center of his messianic mission.

But the cross is not only the outcome of Jesus' conflict with Israel. The cross also reveals the unbroken nature of Jesus' identification with his people and the absoluteness of his will for their redemption. In the face of rejection and the threat of death Jesus does not abandon Israel and found his own sect, or withdraw to the wilderness with the disciple band. His will that all Israel be reconciled with God, and his absolute confidence in the redemptive will of his Father gives him the messianic freedom to carry out his mission even into death. Jesus dies on the cross not simply because his career brought him into conflict with his community, but because he remained true to an unreconciled Israel and to his confidence in the redemptive nearness of God. The "inner" explanation of the cross then is Jesus' "will-to-love" or his "will-to-reconcile" Israel to God.[33]

Above all, the inner root of the cross was Jesus' love for God. The cross is a task he receives from the Father, and is an offering of love and obedience he offers to the Father. In that he accepts the cross he shows how utterly he is bound to the Father, and how freely and absolutely he wills to do what the Father wills. His living for Israel and his dying for Israel, then, both have the same inner root. It is in the cross then that Jesus is revealed as one whose life is determined solely by his will to offer God his obedience, and by his will to restore Israel by offering God's gracious reign to them. The cross is the culminating messianic act of Jesus which discloses that he acts solely as the Son empowered by God to offer redemption. In the cross the sonship of Jesus becomes historically and objectively observable.[34]

The Resurrected Jesus and the Apostolic Testimony

The first volume of Schlatter's New Testament theology, *Die Geschichte des Christus*, concludes with his account of "The Easter story". Under the fairly unfortunate sub-title of, "The continuation of the story of Jesus beyond his end" (*Die Fortsetzung der Geschichte Jesu über sein Ende heraus*) Schlatter portrays the resurrection of Jesus as the final event in his treatment of Jesus' history.[35] It is only *after* the easter event is portrayed that he will turn to the second volume of his New Testament theology, *Die Theologie der Apostel.*[36]

It should be evident that Schlatter's decision to include the resurrection in his account of the story of Jesus, rather than in his account of the witness of the apostles to Jesus, is rather significant. That means that he does not regard the resurrection as something supra-historical, or as a vision or an apostolic conviction that arose in response to the "life-act" of Jesus. He deals with the resurrection as an observable historical event and as an integral part of Jesus' "life-act". That does not mean that the resurrection is observable and comprehensible in a simple empirical way. It is not a brute "fact" that can be established through some quantitative method. But it is observable and comprehensible when seen in continuity with the logic of Jesus' earthly life which was determined and guided by his messianic will. Schlatter writes, "A relationship to the resurrected One can arise in no other way than through a knowledge of his earthly work."[37] Since the disciples knew him in life, and since they were already able to perceive in some fashion that Jesus saw the cross as a messianic act, they are able to now recognize and interpret the resurrection as a part of a whole "life-act". This does not mean that the resurrection does not add anything new to their understanding. Their pre-resurrection understanding was unclear and mixed with uncertainty, and it is only in the resurrection that the messianic character of the cross is clearly established and the Sonship of Jesus is manifest in glory. The cross by its very nature is a mystery. It is victory in defeat; glory in humiliation. It is in the resurrection that the full mystery of defeat and victory in the cross can be comprehended and proclaimed. It is only through the resurrection that the entire "life-act" of the Christ can be seen as the source of a new faith certainty that can become the basis of a new community's life.[38]

The resurrection is also observable as an event not only in relation to the life of Jesus, but also in relation to the life of the new community. For Schlatter the definitive proof that Jesus' life is a messianic act is that it creates a new community. That is evident already in his calling of the disciples. But only in the light of their experience of the resurrection could the disciples confidently call the whole world to be reconciled to God through the cross of Jesus. If we observe the new confidence of the disciples in God's grace for all humankind, and their confident exaltation of Jesus as lord of a new community and the creator of new life, the resurrection immediately becomes visible as the ground of that singular confidence.[39]

Schlatter's confidence that the resurrection is historically observable and even verifiable rests, then, largely on the internal coherence of the story. The resurrection is the only reality that can allow the historian to rigorously follow through on the law of historical continuity. Without the resurrection as an actual event the historian is left with an inexplicable gap in the story. The inner logic of the story will not allow any other interpretation. That inner logic can be described in various ways; I will describe two:

First, there could not be some religious or inner reality that the disciples had apart from the resurrection which subsequently generated easter story legends. To postulate an easter "faith" which gave rise to an easter legend is, in Schlatter's opinion, an utterly fantastic notion.[40] There is no way to move from the story of Jesus as the crucified to Jesus the lord and creator of the new community if the imagination of the disciples is the only vehicle for the transition. The character of the apostolic witness to the resurrection does not point to the intensity of their experience, nor to the strength of their convictions about the resurrection. The affirmation of the resurrection is directed solely toward the person of the resurrected One and away from the subjectivity of those who experienced it. It is presented as something that has been experienced and as an event with actual creative power to ground and establish faith.

Second, were the easter story a product of the disciple's inner life they would have generated a religion of inner fellowship with the resurrected. But the disciples proclaim the resurrection as an act of God that changes history. They proclaim the universal lordship of the glorified Son and announce him as the creator of the community of faith. The resurrection, were it merely a vision, would not impinge on the created sphere of life so Jesus could not become the lord and creator of the new community.[41] In the claim that Jesus is lord, the community attributes to him not only a special metaphysical union with God, but the attributes of God as creator.

Schlatter sees then in the apostolic testimony and in the church that it gave rise to a continuation of the story; of the "life-act" of the Christ. Through the gift of the Spirit and the mediation of the apostolic testimony to Christ, Jesus still meets the community as the living messianic act of God. In him they still are called to repentance and are offered God's grace as forgiveness and as creative power. Schlatter's work in *Die Theologie der Apostel*, is an attempt to trace out with the same methods and rigor that he used in his study of Jesus, how the messianic life-act of the Christ is the sole reality that gives form and content to apostolic theology. The apostles do not merely repeat the Jesus story. They amplify and interpret it for the life of the church, but always with the goal that the distinctive life-act of the Christ be represented and formed in the community of faith. Schlatter finds confirmation of the truth of the Jesus story in the fact that even where the disciples do not quote or follow the outlines of the Jesus story; even where they use their freedom and imagination to go beyond the received story, their thought is still imprinted with the form of the messianic life-act of the Christ.[42] The authenticity of the apostolic calling is partly manifest in the very freedom with which the apostolic witnesses expand on such topics as the pre-existence of the Christ, or on how he received his commissioning from the Father, or how his work continues on in glory. The apostolic witness is united in its goal of carrying on the messianic will of Jesus, but it contains diversity in that each apostolic witness speaks out of their own history and addresses a distinct community of faith. The witnesses are under obligation to follow the rule of truth and present Jesus alone, but they are also free to use their own stock of inherited ideas and their own imaginations to extend the continuing messianic work further.

In perhaps what is one of Schlatter's most eloquent phrases he describes the task and the position of the apostolic witnesses:

> With all the uncertainties of his historical memory and his prophetic foresight, the biblical narrator is the servant of God, who awakens the memory of him and makes known his will. If he does not do it as who knows, then he does it as one who dreams. If his eye fails then the imagination enters in and fills the necessary holes. Even in this way he ushers forward the divine gift which has entered into the course of history, and makes it fruitful for later generations. That he is called to serve God not only as one who knows and thinks but also as one who dreams and composes, is grounded in the fact that he is a person, and we human beings cannot arrest the transition from thought to poetry; to require such would be to strive against the given conditions of our humanness.[43]

The story of Jesus continues "beyond his end" not merely in the apostolic teaching. More important it continues on in the very life of the church. Jesus continues to be revealed as the messiah because he continues to create a community that is united through faith in him; and he continues to recreate the community as a people whose will and action is one with his. The central theme of Schlatter's ecclesiology is that the church is not called simply to a "thought religion", or to be a community that cherishes certain beliefs about Jesus. Rather the church is called into an active fellowship of will and action with its lord. The church of the New Testament is truly called to be the continuation of the life-act of the Christ.

Some Questions about Schlatter's Method

The critical reader of Schlatter's depiction of "the story of Jesus", cannot help but raise the question of his "naivete". New Testament scholarship since Schlatter's time has so thoroughly documented the role of the post-resurrection community in the shaping of the Jesus story that we are deeply aware of that question every time we read our scriptures. Does not Schlatter's straightforward account of the story of Jesus obscure the extent to which that story is the creation of the early church? And along with that doesn't he cover up the real tension that remains between the Jesus of history and the Christ, or even the Christ$_s$ of faith?

This question needs to be answered on a couple of different levels. The first is that Schlatter is *not* unaware of the gaps in our historical understanding of Jesus and of the creative role the Christian community plays in portraying the "life-act" of the Christ. He has a historical epistemology which is broad enough to accommodate that fact. The messianic character of Jesus is not established primarily by establishing as historical fact the claim that Jesus himself used messianic titles (though Schlatter argues he did), but that the entire Jesus story portrays him as one who *acts* with messianic *authority*. If one counters that by saying that it was the early apostolic community that portrayed Jesus as acting with messianic authority because of their conviction that he was the messiah, then Schlatter would respond that that is a poor historical judgment. The Jesus story so understood would be unintelligible because it would violate the rule of historical continuity. The New Testament, nor anything else for that matter, does not give us any explanation for how the early church could be the generative ground for giving rise to the conviction that Jesus is the messiah. The theory that Jesus is portrayed as messiah only because the apostolic community came to the conviction that he was the messiah leaves two great gaps in our understanding of the New Testament. It leaves us not knowing who Jesus really was and why it was he who was thus honored by the church, and it leaves us not knowing by what process the early church came to share and live by this conviction.

Schlatter, however, would not deny that the Jesus of the New Testament is seen by us only as the apostolic community experienced and portrayed him. This is how it should be. The "life-act" of the Christ is not comprehended apart from the effect it had on those who by faith became participants in it. The "real" Jesus is for Schlatter the Jesus who lives on in the community of faith whose subsequent history takes form around and in some ways gives form to the life that created it and is still being lived out in it. Word and Spirit, faith and history are interwoven in the story of the Christ and mutually condition one another.

But having shown (once again) that Schlatter is not naive, and that his epistemology is cognizant of the role of the church in shaping the story of Jesus, it must be added that we are still left with some questions over the adequacy of his treatment. For Schlatter history and story in the New Testament are virtually one. Even if one goes with him in acknowledging that there is no need for an absolute distinction between story and history, still one is left with the distinction, and it is hard to see how a modern historian could help but remain aware of it. Just because the Jesus story is internally coherent; just because it portrays a man who lives his life in and from God, who knows himself to be called to offer forgiveness and salvation to Israel, and who through his cross and resurrection God calls a new community of faith into being; does that establish all the elements of the story as history? For example, does it establish that Jesus actually interacted with John the Baptist, an interaction that Schlatter exhaustively analyzes, or might not the New Testament give attention to that interaction because the community needed to sort out how it should relate to John's disciples? One could affirm the latter and still believe that the biblical accounts of the interaction of Jesus and John is the work of Spirit in the community as it continues to live out the "life-act" of the Christ. But then one would also have to acknowledge that those accounts are not "history" as we commonly use the word today.

It would appear that even if one were to endorse Schlatter's emphasis on the "life-act" of Jesus, and accept his philosophy of history in which story and history are not totally separate realities, one would still have to say that his method tends to blunt vigorous historical critical investigation, and a more adequate historical method would need to make room for a more pointed and critical investigation of the historicity of the story. Or perhaps we could say, it would need to work at being clear and specific on just how the social and theological context of the early apostolic communities are reflected in their telling of the Jesus story. This would seem to conform to Schlatter's own rule of historical continuity. Attention to how the social and theological context of the early church formed their retelling of the Jesus story could become an important aspect of a broader understanding of the story of the Christ.

Another important question to put to Schlatter is how the historian can move from a phenomenological description of how the early church experienced Jesus, or even how Jesus experienced himself to a normative historical judgment. It may well be true that Jesus carried within himself an unshakable certainty that he was called to offer salvation to Israel, and it may be true that it is this certainty which is determinative of his entire "life-act", but can that in itself lead the historian to the judgment that Jesus is messiah? It would appear that historical judgment which Schlatter finds to be the only compelling scientific decision available is indistinguishable from what is normally called "faith". But can Schlatter hope to explain how the mind makes the transition from a descriptive grasp of the Jesus story to a normative judgment of faith in Jesus as messiah? This appears, for better or worse, to be the outcome of his historical methodology.

Endnotes

1.*Die Religionswissenschaft der Gegenwart im Selbstdarstellungen*, ed. D. Erich Stange (Leipzig: Felix Meiner Verlag, 1925), 153.

2.*Briefe über Das Christliche Dogma* (Stuttgart: Calwer Verlag, 2nd. ed., 1978) #11. Schlatter sees the need to explain things in terms of cause and effect as an intellectual "given" that is planted in our lives by God the creator.

3.Schlatter's understanding of history and the nature of historical events will be explained further in ch. V–VII. Especially in ch. VI we will explain how for Schlatter, a historical event is never fully understood by a study of the "objective" or external historical happening in and of itself. Events must also be understood in relation to the subjectivity of the historical actors and in relation to the subjectivity of the historical interpreter. In Schlatter's thought there are certain "laws" or regularities that characterize "personal life" (*Leben*) and these must enter into the process of understanding historical events. That means then that history is not the record of *wie es eigentlich gewesen sei*, rather it is the living effects of an event as it was experienced and mediated to us through human participants in those events.

4.*Rückblick auf meine Lebensarbeit*, 233.

5.Schlatter was quite aware of the "historical Jesus" quest and concept and brusquely rejected it. To him a search for a Jesus who existed prior to or apart from the apostolic witness to Jesus is the quest for an unhistorical abstraction, and the search itself reveals a misguided understanding of historical methodology.

6.Ibid., 233-234.

7.When translating Schlatter there is no great difference whether one decides to translate "*Geschichte*" as "history" or "story". If one means by "history" a presentation of the facts as they are ascertainable by historical science, then clearly that is not what Schlatter means by the phrase "*die Geschichte Jesu*", or "*Die Geschichte des Christus*". If one means by story a fanciful narrative whose value is independent of its historical truthfulness, then Schlatter does not intend that meaning either. For him history is both historical event and narrative imagination which interprets and extends a historical event. For Schlatter the narrative line of the entire New Testament *is* the story of the historical Jesus.

8.We come here again to the role of Schlatter's anthropology and his concept of "personal life" in relationship to his understanding of historical method. Schlatter's concept of personal life needs to be systematically developed as a tool for the "scientific" study of history. History is unintelligible apart from a knowledge of what personal life is and how it is lived in and through history. This of course raises the question of whether Schlatter truly finds a unity in the New Testament or whether he does finally harmonize the New Testament by imposing his systematic anthropology upon it.

9.One might add that for Schlatter it does not matter whether Jesus is portrayed as the individual hero because of Romantic notions about the creative "genius", or because of the orthodox notion of the deity of Jesus. Whether Jesus' unique individuality is immanently or supernaturalistically explained such a view destroys the unity and intelligibility of his "life-act".

10.*Der Glaube im Neuen Testament*, 231.

11.Johannes Heinrich Schmid, *Erkenntnis des geschichtlichen Christus bei Martin Kähler und bei Adolf Schlatter*, Theologische Zeitschrift, Sonderband V (Basel: Friedrich Reinhardt Verlag, 1978).

12.The term *Gewißheit*, here rendered as "certainty" is a word fraught with theological significance throughout Schlatter's works. This "certainty" is for him more than a subjective attitude of confidence. It is a term that expresses the anthropological co-ordinates of faith. "Certainty" is what the creative grace of God creates within the believer's "personal- life" and is descriptive of what governs the believers relationship with God.

13.The first edition of Schlatter's New Testament theology was bound in one volume entitled *Theologie des Neuen Testaments*. Within that single volume there were two sections; the first entitled "Das Wort Jesu" and the second, "Die Theologie der Apostel". In the second edition Schlatter changed the title of the first section to, "Die Geschichte des Christus". The reason that he gives for the change in his *Rückblick auf meine Lebensarbeit* (p. 231), is that the former title tended to perpetuate the intellectual tradition which separated word from deed, and which made the formal "teachings" of Jesus the basis of theology.

14.See *Die Geschichte des Christus*, pp. 33–41 and 270 –304 for Schlatter's discussion of Jesus in relationship to Israel.

15.Ibid., 291.

16.Ibid., 36, 150.

17.Ibid., 143 –144.

18.See our discussion in Ch. VI. p. 115.

19.*Die Geschichte des Christus*, from the 'Foreword', 5.

20.Ibid., 7.

21.Ibid., 121.

22."Der Zweifel an der Messianität Jesu", 154.

23.Ibid.

24.Ibid., 155.

25.Ibid.

26.Ibid., 165.

27.Ibid., 160.

28.Schlatter always insists that the conflict of Jesus with the Pharisees was not "political", nor was it only "theological". But of course to say something is "not political" means only as much as what you do or do not mean by the word "political". When Schlatter says Jesus is "not political" he means that Jesus is not motivated by the will to displace the religious rulers of Israel so that he could rule in their place. But the conflict *is* political in that he seeks to claim all of Israel's life for God alone. It is important to note that for Schlatter the conflict is *not* over who had the right doctrines or even over whether Christ had a special status which enabled him to reveal God; the conflict was over whether or not Jesus' claim to rulership over Israel on God's behalf was justified.

29.Ibid., 163.

30.*Der Glaube im Neuen Testament*, 321.

31.*Die Geschichte des Christus*, 108.

32.Ibid., 452.

33.Ibid., 458.

34.Ibid., 460. I have followed Schlatter's presentation of Jesus' career as a thoroughly messianic event. He also gives extensive attention to Jesus as the Son, and roots messianic activity in Jesus' consciousness of his divine Sonship. For Schlatter sonship is not a metaphysical substance, but is at heart a "community of wills" (*Willens-gemeinschaft*), or a community of love that is actualized in the messianic acts of Jesus. I have developed the messianic theme rather the that of Sonship in order to simplify and shorten my account.

35.*Die Geschichte des Christus*, 517 ff.

36.The distinction Schlatter makes between "the story of Jesus" and "the theology of the apostles" parallels his distinction between New Testament theology and dogmatics. The distinction is relative and functional rather than absolute. He is fully aware that the "historical" Jesus cannot be cleanly lifted out of the apostolic testimony through which Jesus is presented.

37.Ibid., 523.

38.Ibid., 530.

39.Ibid., 531–533.

40.Ibid., 518 –521.

41.Ibid., 534.

42.Ibid., 528–529.

43.*Das Christliche Dogma*, p. 377. This section is quoted with hearty approval by Karl Barth in his discussion of the concept of "Saga" in *Kirchliche Dogmatik*, III, 1, p. 83. (I have used my translation rather than the one given by the English translators of *CD* III, 1.) Barth wants to distinguish biblical narrative from "myth" and "history". But what Barth calls "history" would be what Schlatter would call neo-Kantian classification of data into an immanent time-space manifold; an ahistorical approach to history. Schlatter would not acknowledge that there is something called "history" which historical scientists study, and that then the biblical narrative that theologians interpret is something other than history.

Chapter V

AGAINST ALL "GODLESS" VIEWS OF HISTORY

Up to this point our study has given an impression of how Schlatter approaches historical study of the New Testament and how he portrays the "life-act" of the Christ. We have made allusions to the fact that in the process of "observing" the New Testament Schlatter has developed and made use of a distinctive epistemology, indeed a distinctive philosophy of history. While his concern is to understand the New Testament and the Jesus story, we have suggested that his work is often motivated by a methodological interest as well. Beginning with this chapter we will look more closely and reflectively at his epistemology and display more fully how it is rooted in his understanding of history (Ch. VI), the person (Ch. VII), and the creative character of God's grace (Ch. VIII). One could say that to this point we have been looking at Schlatter the historian; from here on we will be looking more at Schlatter the theologically oriented philosopher of history.

Schlatter rejected the charge that he was a naive biblicist and preferred to call himself a "Kritik der Kritik".[1] And indeed there is an analytical and polemical interest and motive that lies just beneath the surface in his primary biblical studies. These interests receive further development in his methodological and autobiographical essays. His polemics can take the rough form of an outspoken jibe at a thinker or a school of thought. But at times it can be expanded into a sustained and knowledgeable discussion of the thinker or method that he opposes. Schlatter himself worked and thought as a biblical historian and he surveys the history and effects of the western intellectual heritage largely in terms of how it has influenced our view of history, and our understanding of the relationship of God to history. Summarily stated, Schlatter sets himself against all views of history that ignore history in order to know God, or which ignore God in order to understand history. It is this alienation between God and history that he rejects in the name of the God who reveals Himself *in* history and whose revelation is creative *of* history. This chapter will attempt to outline his critique of all "Godless" views of history beginning with his broad philosophical criticisms and leading up to his discussions of how historical methodology has been hindered by these views.

It should be stated at the outset that our discussion in this chapter will stress the polemical side of Schlatter's philosophical discussions, and that is the case because our study focuses on the philosophy of history. Schlatter's general attitude toward philosophy is not simply polemical, nor does he believe that philosophy has no bearing on theology. For him the philosophical heritage and discipline is an essential discussion partner for the dogmatic theologian. In his view philosophy is a vital human activity which is motivated by our desire for truth and understanding, and by our innate awareness of the question of God.[2] And as we will note later in our discussion of his theological anthropology, Schlatter believes that these motives (the awareness of the truth question and the awareness of God) are firmly rooted in the fact that human beings are products of God's creative work.

Schlatter, in describing his understanding of the relationship of theology and philosophy, chooses to describe them as "parallel" disciplines.[3] He is concerned to maintain the independence and distinctiveness of theology, but not at the expense of severing reciprocal ties with philosophical disciplines. Philosophy contributes to historical and theological studies a concern for intelligibility, causality, unity and finality of understanding that makes a positive contribution. But philosophy is in itself always a helping discipline. A given philosophical concept or system must be judged by its usefulness in helping us to understand human experience. Philosophy does not provide an overarching system within which the theologian must organize truth. The great temptation of philosophy throughout history has been an over fascination with self-contained systems (*"Systembildnerei"*) which are given authority because of their author's name or their rational coherence. For Schlatter there is an essentially pragmatic view of philosophical concepts; that is they are true if they are useful and contribute to the task of "observation". One does not begin the historical or dogmatic component of the theological task by identifying what philosophical presuppositions will be operative, but one begins with a commitment to sober, thorough observation and asks how philosophical tools contribute or detract from the task.[4] Philosophers and philosophical influences need to be evaluated, then, according to their effects in the areas of theory of knowledge, ethics and knowledge of God. And it is from Schlatter's faith stance and his task as a historian and theologian that philosophical tools are viewed and evaluated.

Schlatter's forays into philosophical criticism are the outgrowth of a life-long study and interest in the philosophical heritage. As a student he noted that his first love was philology. And it was the study of philology that contributed to the historicization of his thinking.[5] It was from his background in philology that he moved into the study of philosophy and theology. In an interesting comment on how his philological studies influenced his view of history Schlatter writes:

> Since I came to be a theologian through the guidance of a philologist, I could never have a theology that forgot history, or a history that hid God from me.[6]

The same can be said of his study of philosophy. His philosophical training was done primarily at Berne with Steffensen whose lectures on the history of philosophy he heard for four semesters. The decisive result of his historicized introduction to philosophical studies meant that for him the idea of "pure reason" died forever, and he became a tireless critic of various forms of rationalism and their influence in theology.

As a *Dozent* at the University of Berne Schlatter actually lectured on the history of philosophy, and he continued his philosophical lectures even when he held the chair in New Testament Theology at Tübingen. We have the fruits of his philosophical labors in his 1906 work entitled, "Die philosophische Arbeit seit Cartesius nach ihrem ethischen und religiosen Ertrag".[7] It is here that we find his most sustained philosophical reflections and criticism, especially of German idealism. While our work in this chapter must draw on several sources, this work will provide a primary source for our discussion of his understanding of Descartes, Kant, and Schleiermacher. But it is to his critique of the origins of western rationalism that we must first turn our attention.

Against Greek Rationalism

Schlatter belongs to the generation of scholars who first discovered and developed the idea of a clear distinction between "Hellenistic" and "biblical" modes of thought. He was for a time a colleague of Adolf Harnack at Berlin and spoke very highly of his work in the history of dogma. He reports that he "took a lively interest" in Harnack's attempt to uncover the hellenistic influence in church history and theology.[8]

While Schlatter has no sustained discussion of Plato or Aristotle, nor a detailed critique of their influence on theology, passing references to the Greek heritage abound. In short, his criticism of Greek rationalism is that it separates the act of thinking from other aspects of human life, and gives the intellect and ideas a priority that is not true to human experience. For example, in a comment in his *Briefe über Das Christliche Dogma*, he makes reference to the greek tradition that persists on through Kant, whereby the intellectual apprehension of an idea is separated from the sensual apprehension of the object.[9] That entails that the evidence of our senses is a secondary and inferior way of knowing, and that pure intellectual activity is something wholly separable and essentially independent from experience. In Schlatter's understanding that separates and alienates two human functions that belong together. The intellect is not capable of understanding apart from the function of the human senses, and the human senses require intellectual awareness and activity. To separate the intellect from experience is to cut ourselves off from the knowledge of reality and to limit ourselves to the realm of unproductive abstractions. Abstractions, in Schlatter's understanding, have no potency or capability to establish experience; in fact it is experience which must give content and actuality to abstractions.[10]

In his *Briefe über das Christliche Dogma*, Schlatter has a sharp statement and criticism of the greek and rationalistic idea of knowledge:

> I have rejected the greek and rationalistic description of humanity. My counter-thesis runs: our consciousness as it is formed in conjunction with our life-act is always formed, is always continuously conditioned not by empty, but rather by filled concepts. We possess no other knowledge than concepts which emerge from singular experiences. What the rationalists denigrate as "the accidental truths of history", that is our entire spiritual heritage![11]

Schlatter's critique of essential rationalism is two-fold; it is both anthropological and theological. The anthropological critique is essentially personalistic. That is for Schlatter, the careful observation of how we think and come to understand (as opposed to theoretical constructions of how understanding takes place) shows that understanding is an integrated personal act. The human person is not primarily a disembodied intellect but a person with a personal history and a distinctive way of acting and viewing the world. Schlatter's rather strange assertion is that thinking begins with the eye; or at least that it is the eye that awakens thought. And the eye (or how we view the world) is shaped by the conventions of history, language and culture. Our ability to think is given to us as a part of our cultural and linguistic heritage. So thought is from the beginning historically conditioned.

At yet another level beyond the cultural and linguistic conventions that are the givens of a certain time and place, the individual's intellect is also shaped by their feelings and by their will and prior actions. Action itself has a kind of intellectual potency which opens up or closes certain avenues of thought. In short, it is inevitably a person who thinks, therefore the intellectual function is distinct but never wholly separable from the "life act" of the thinker.[12]

The theological critique of Greek rationalism again centers on the
autonomy and primacy of the intellect and the effect that that has had on the
church's self-understanding. With regards to the scriptures, rationalism
established itself clearly in the synagogue and especially in the work of
Philo, and from there was taken over by the church. The result is that the
scriptures came to be seen in a one-sided way as a medium of knowledge,
and the inspiration of scripture came to refer to their utter reliability and
accuracy as a medium of knowledge.[13] Another aspect of greek intellectual-
ism that Schlatter does battle with is the primacy of the intellect over the
will in the area of ethics. This understanding of ethics has meant that in
biblical studies theologians often misunderstand Jesus and his uniqueness.
Since Jesus is generally regarded as a bearer of a unique message, or as
God's representative, theology mistakenly looks for the new concept of God
that Jesus brings, or for the new theological ideas he espouses which
transcend his Jewishness. In Schlatter's opinion that is fruitless. Jesus taught
nothing new. Were we to study his theology or his ethics we would learn
only what the Judaism of the day taught about theology and ethics. Jesus'
uniqueness, and his function as God's representative is in his address to the
will. He called Israel to repentance and a new trust in the nearness of God.

As is perhaps fairly predictable, Schlatter goes on to argue that this
greek heritage intellectualized the church's life and self-understanding. The
church came to be identified and recognized primarily by what it taught and
believed, rather than by its activity. Its teachings became formalized in
doctrines and in formal creeds that had the force of law in the thought of the
church, and faith became the intellectual affirmation of the church's
teachings. In Schlatter's opinion even the Reformers did not adequately
address the problem of an intellectualized faith. While Luther's genius was
that he clearly put his faith in Jesus and not in doctrine, it is still not
adequately clear in the Lutheran heritage that one is not justified by
intellectual agreement with the concept of justification. Schlatter even wants
to argue that Luther's emphasis on the utter passivity of faith is indirectly

a product of the intellectualist heritage, in that it separates the mental activity of having faith from the volitional life of the believer.

For Schlatter the church's historic credalism, and what he regarded as the consequent intellectualizing of faith, is a significant factor which bars our access to the New Testament. It leads us away from the historical concreteness and personhood of Jesus and toward a faith system which can best be understood by further intellectual reflection and clarification of church doctrine. It leads us away from the concrete historical mediation of the apostolic community and toward an ahistorical view of scripture as a medium of knowledge. And perhaps above all it leads us away from a New Testament understanding of faith as the creative work of God to create a community of love and obedience, and leads toward faith as the intellectual acquiescence of the individual to the formal teachings of the church.

Against Cartesianism

While Schlatter may identify the greek rationalists as the root of all rationalisms, it is really with Descartes that he begins his discussion of how rationalism has influenced the modern view of history and historical method. Descartes renounced his former education and the opinions of all other people from the past and present in order to use pure reason to establish undubitable truth based on the ideal of mathematical certainty. His goal was to purify reason absolutely.

There are three aspects of Descartes' thought that Schlatter denotes as the typical marks of his approach and which have had far reaching effects on subsequent thought. The first is his attempt to ground knowledge in unrestrained doubt; the second, his focus on the individual thinker in and of himself; and the third, the attempt to establish certainty through pure thought itself.[14] I will address his evaluation of each of these three characteristics in order.

First, Schlatter notes that the elevation of doubt to a methodological principle is a clear reversal of most previous thought. At least in western

Christendom, belief was regarded as the normal state of mind and as the best guide to understanding, while doubt was viewed as an aberration. In a sense, Descartes, too, was aware of the aberrant character of doubt and never adopted it as an end in itself. It was intended to serve only as a means to attaining certainty. At that point the vehicle of doubt would be discarded. And yet, in Schlatter's opinion, it is perhaps not actually that simple. A radical change in one's intellectual procedures inevitably has an effect on ethical values and religious outlook. Once again, the thought-act is inseparable from the totality of the person who is doing the thinking.

Descartes' favorable evaluation of doubt is possible only through an attempt to separate doubt as an intellectual activity from other aspects of personal life. However, Schlatter's suggestion is that inevitably the decision to use whatever means are necessary, including radical doubt, to advance the cause of knowledge implies that any activity or approach which has the result of increasing knowledge is desirable and good. The quest for intellectual mastery has been set up as an end in itself, and an activity such as radical doubt, which could be destructive of religious and moral values is given a privileged status because it serves the goal of knowing. So even though it appears to have only a penultimate value as a means to an end, in another sense it has established itself as the supreme value and activity in and of itself. Schlatter suggests that the sign that doubt itself has triumphed as a value in itself is the exaltation of the "free-thinker" type who is regarded as a great thinker not because of fruitful results or actual wisdom, but because of the unrestrained determination to doubt.

However, the ease with which Descartes can overcome his initial unrestricted doubt shows that his doubting was actually based on an underlying confidence.[15] Actually, his doubt was a device. It served to free him from traditional ideas and from the previous results of science, but it did not erode his essential confidence in ideas and in science itself. He doubted the previous achievements of reason, but he never brought himself to doubt reason itself. So in a sense, Locke and Hume are more critical than Descartes was, and Kant more critical again than the English empiricists.

Schlatter's understanding is that Descartes essentially used doubt to free himself from authority and the traditions of the past in order to establish the isolated thinker as the source of truth:

> Through doubting he was able to establish the independence of his own thought over against the entire stock of ideas that history has offered to us.[16]

The second characteristic of Descartes' thought, the isolation of the individual thinker in and of himself, is the product of the principle of doubt. The principle of doubt isolates the thinker from other people and from history in order to find certainty in and through itself:

> How does Descartes end the conflict that he began within himself through doubting? The thinker finds the means within himself in that he separates himself from community, isolates himself from history and creates for himself a complete self-reliance. Descartes was always suspicious of history because it could only create misunderstanding, it could only enslave the thinker. He boldly put forward the isolated self over against the common life. The self needs no teachers, it requires no receptivity or experiences; it simply thinks and creates through thought that which the community could never offer to it; namely, truth.[17]

In other words, Descartes' influence has tended to sever the individual thinker from the common life and from the giving and receiving that Schlatter believes is essential to human life and therefore to human thought. In Descartes the individual thinker is in himself creative of knowledge and certainty prior to any act of receptivity be it toward history, other people, nature or God. Philosophy then is a discipline which is the story of singular biographies. It is the story of isolated thinkers who reject the past and heroically determine to start thinking anew. Schlatter also points out, however, that this ideal is in a sense historically unrealizable. Even the great geniuses form "schools" which are an acknowledgement of the need for community and for giving and receiving in order for knowledge to be advanced.

Schlatter correlates this emphasis on the isolated individual thinker with the rise of the concept that the primary task of the philosopher is to overcome "prejudice" (*Vorurteil*) and to begin totally anew with the intellectual enterprise.[18] The attack on "prejudice" assumes that the key to thought, or at least the essential prerequisite to pure reason was to clear the mind of all that it had received through language, culture, tradition and history.

As such Cartesianism is in Schlatter's view a massive "protest against history".[19] It turned not only against the recent past of the Middle Ages as had Humanism, but it turned also against the ancient heritage of the Greeks. Schlatter takes delight in pointing up what he finds to be a real irony of this protest against history, and that is that Descartes himself clearly demonstrates he is not free of history, especially the greek heritage. History cannot and should not be cleanly broken out of in order for thought to be pure. Schlatter's commentary is:

> History consists of real interconnections that are just as unbreakable as those that we find in nature. Descartes himself experienced this. The observation on which he fell back was "I think", and at that point he believed he had grasped his own existence and concluded from that that the essence of his soul was the activity of thinking. But that was not a new idea. The proposition that the creation of ideas constitutes the most deeply characteristic mark of the human essence; the idea that "Reason" is the most real and the best of what it means to be human is a hellenistic inheritance. Descartes failed to see that his own consciousness, that on which he ultimately relied, had a particular determinative form that had been given to him by history. So then he was not pure reason, but was that which his position in history had made him to be.[20]

Third, Descartes' ideal was pure reason, and true to the ancient ideal "pure" reason is reason functioning in complete independence from the senses and from human experience. This ancient ideal is renewed and strengthened in Descartes' era by the remarkable results produced from the mathematicization of nature. Schlatter argues that it was the success of mathematics in understanding and controlling nature that undergirded the entire wider movement of rationalism.

The ideal of pure reason had profound effects in the area of religion. Schlatter points out that in the attempt to separate reason from other human functions, reason was also separated from feeling or passion.[21] So whereas intellectual work in the church had always been characterized by the greatest of passions, pure reason should be free of the same. In the church a conflict of ideas inevitably brought human beings into conflict because it dealt with matters of deep personal and eternal importance. Given the history of the church's conflicts and unresolved arguments, a pure affectless reasoning process appears to be an ethical improvement and a liberating force.

Schlatter makes a subtle but critical point in his critique of Descartes, that again leads to his main point that Cartesianism separates us from history. Descartes, through his exercise in doubt, has become aware that he as a thinking subject exists. But he misinterprets this awareness in two ways. First, he believes that his intellect created this certainty through its own creative activity. But in actuality what his exercise has done is simply made him aware of something that is a part of and arises out of "the given form of our life".[22] His "I am" is not founded by his intellectual endeavor so that in as much as he thinks he is, rather his exercise has uncovered an awareness of existence and self-hood that is an essential part of personal life. He concludes wrongly then, that his existence consists in his thinking, whereas in actuality his thinking is grounded in the given-ness of his personal-life and is one unique expression of self-hood.

Second, he mistakenly believes that since his own existence is indubitable he has arrived at "a clear and distinct idea". But Schlatter suggests that even though this awareness is indubitable it is by no means "clear and distinct". Once one begins to reflect on the activity of thinking and being, and why we are compelled to think and how it is related to our being, one begins to realize that we stand before an inexhaustible puzzle. It is Descartes' tenet that we can only affirm that which is exhaustively comprehensible by a "clear and distinct idea". But Schlatter asserts that both nature and history confront us with many things that demand to be acknowledged and affirmed even though they are mysterious to the core and cannot be exhaustively comprehended. So once again Cartesianism is a protest against history and against the given-ness of our experience:

When the Cartesian canon is so interpreted as to mean that we may only affirm that we which we have conceptually comprehended, then such a rationalism must find itself immediately in a fierce struggle with nature and history. There is much in nature and history that continually demands our acknowledgement and affirmation, and which determine our lives with the undeniable force of reality, even though they remain an unfathomable mystery to us.[23]

The Theological Effects of Cartesianism

Cartesian rationalism, in Schlatter's opinion, had left a decisive mark on theology even up to his day. In his complete separation of thought from experience Descartes prepared the way for a clean division between reason and faith, or between rational and revealed theology. After him there are two types of theology, one rational and one historical, that exist along side one another.[24] Since pure reason deals with universal and necessary truths and revealed theology must work with the material of history, its outcomes must always appear to be of particular and contingent interest rather than of universal value. Since to think (for a rationalist) means to think as a Cartesian, the validity and integrity of revealed theology becomes questionable. While the Cartesian God is an idea the truth of which is proven because it is logically necessary for the system of ideas to be complete, the church's knowledge of God is mediated through scripture and the faith and experience of prior generations. Therefore, the church's understanding of God belongs to the realm of that which is dubitable, questionable and confused. A historical religion begins to appear more as something that is arbitrary. Its truth value cannot be reasonably affirmed so it can only be affirmed on the basis of authoritarianism, or through some other human function which is unrelated to reason.

While Descartes seemed content to let these two forms of theology co-exist side by side, in practice that is never quite possible. Given the already long standing rationalism in theology, revealed theology tended to adopt the ideals and procedures of a rational theology. Rational theology with its proofs and its logical necessity came to have the upper-hand. In Schlatter's evaluation that means that a theology which is reduced to abstractions and syllogisms won the upper-hand over a faith filled with all the riches of historical tradition.[25] Or one other result was the creation of a theology that accepted the Cartesian definition of reason but then gloried in the need for a faith that is beyond reason and which can only base itself on a decision of the will. This kind of faith sees the unreasonableness of faith, or the uncertainty of faith as the essential mark of faith (as opposed to other forms of knowledge). So from Descartes on their is a kind of theology that regards scepticism as a servant of faith. In this approach:

> ...scepticism serves as the basis of faith. A believing heart should be accompanied by a heathen head, while faith and atheistic science should somehow co-exist in the same person.[26]

Finally, another result of Cartesian rationalism is that the person effectively disappears from his thought. One reason for this is that reason separates itself totally from nature. Nature is simply extended matter which can be mathematically quantified. For Schlatter this mathematicization of nature is an expression of power and domination over nature. Nature is subordinated to mathematics which is a human capacity, so the richness of nature disappears behind our intellectual idealization of it. This has profound effects for our understanding of ourselves and God. It obscures the fact that we are a part of nature and that our attitude toward it cannot simply be one of mastery and control, but also one of receptivity. The gifts and faculties we have as human beings are given to us by nature, so our first task is to receive from nature with respect and humility.

This also effects our knowledge of God because essential to our knowledge of God is our awareness of Him as creator.[27] The Cartesian God created a world of extended matter, and the mathematical laws that guide them. That view of nature is incompatible with the biblical idea of God created personhood which is capable and called to respond to God not only with the intellect, but the will, and with passion as well. To begin with an exaggerated and untruthful separation of thought from other aspects of personal life is finally to destroy the person and even to destroy the capacity for knowing truth for which the intellect is intended. A massive protest against nature and history is finally destructive of the person because nature and history are God's gifts which give us the conditions which make personal life a possibility.

Against Kantianism

If there is a philosopher with whom Schlatter is pre-occupied it is certainly Immanuel Kant. References to Kant can be found throughout his methodological essays, and he devotes a major portion of his philosophical writing to a direct treatment of Kant. In Schlatter's view it is Kant who completely dominated german philosophy, theology and even historical scholarship right up to his own time. But he is also interested in neo-Kantianism and its wide spread influence especially in the area of historical research and biblical studies. His position relative to Kant is not easily classified. He respects his criticism of the Cartesian dogma of pure reason, but he levels all his criticisms against rationalism in general at Kant in particular. He regularly attacks Kant for his subject centered approach to knowledge, yet he acknowledges in his *Briefe über das Christliche Dogma*, that he shares in common with Kant the realization that a theory of knowledge and our understanding of truth and error must arise out of the inner life of the person![28]

Schlatter's discussion of Kant is wide-ranging and deals with his influence on ethics, theory of knowledge, and our concept of God. We will need to limit our discussion here somewhat and give a generalized overview of his critique of Kant, and then give more close attention to Kant's influence in the area of theory of knowledge and how that has effected biblical studies and theology.

In Schlatter's opinion Kant had reached to the very heart of the basic epistemological question. To Schlatter any attempt to address the most basic questions of our life leads us into "impenetrable mysteries"; mysteries that can be explored but never exhaustively comprehended.[29] Though Kant is critical of the unchastened rational dogmatism of a Descartes, it is clear to Schlatter that Kant's faith in "pure reason" continues unbroken. As in

Descartes the ideal of mathematics is the model for all knowledge; even knowledge of other persons, ethics and God. Kant's confidence in "pure reason" is displayed in the fact that he does not ask *if* we form synthetic a priori judgments, rather he asks only *how* we form them. He is certain that the only knowledge available is that which the subject forms for itself out of its own synthetic use of pure reason. So in as much as the philosopher clarifies how pure reason can form knowledge, he both establishes the validity of that knowledge *as well as* shows us the clear and inviolable limits of that knowledge.[30] You might say then that Schlatter would compliment Kant on his awareness of the problematic nature of pure reason, and on his realization that the prior question is that of how human experience is even a possibility at all. But where Schlatter will criticize him (at times even excoriate him!) is that instead of actually *observing* human experience to see how it is that human knowledge actually takes place, Kant uses reason to analyze the idea of experience and thus determines dogmatically just how knowledge may and may not occur. Kant uses speculative reason, not "observation" of "realities" to secure his insights.

For Kant what the self knows it produces out of itself. There is no concept of the persons dependence on experience, or culture or history. The self remains a "leibnizian monad" that generates understanding from itself and is essentially independent of all experience.[31] Reason contains the pure forms of perception, so all of our experiences appear in time and space; it contains the categories of understanding such as unity, causality and substance, so all of our experience appears to us as a unified field of things linked together in causal relationships; and reason generates our ideas of a self, of the world and God as necessary by-products of the operation of reason. But the price Kant pays for this redemption of pure reason is high; he loses the world. Both the world of nature and the reality of the individual self become unknowable and are reduced to the status of "appearances".

The self in Kant, is not only unknowable, it is displaced by an abstraction. When Kant speaks of thought or reason he can never speak of the empirical individual or the person who does the thinking. Reason is,

..."a hypostasized abstraction; an abstraction masquerading as a reality." Kant never stops to ask the question of just where this thing called "reason" is or where it has come from. Kant is, "...one of the most noteworthy examples of how an abstraction can come to be regarded as a reality... Attention to abstractions entirely replaces the observing of reality."[32]

Schlatter's main concern in discussing Kant is to trace out the influences of his thought. He sees three distinct phases in the development of Kantianism. The first is the philosophy of Kant itself and the reaction from his contemporaries. The second stage is that of the great Kantian philosophers; Fichte, Schelling, Hegel and Schopenhauer to name the best known. All of them stand within the Kantian framework and seek to carry philosophy further given that starting point. We will not trace out Schlatter's discussion of this group except to note that he believes their disagreements, failures and dogmatism adequately demonstrate the impotence of abstractions. Each is dogmatic because each can only assume that universal pure reason, not empirical individuals, speak through them.

But the third and most important stage of the development of Kantianism follows the breakdown of this second speculative stage, and is essentially the triumph of Kantian scepticism:

> Then came the collapse of the speculative continuation of Kantianism and with it came a movement back to Kant. But not back to his ethic but rather to his critical theses regarding the limited powers of reason. These became the common property of the educated. They became detached from their ground in Kant's overall philosophy and spread out as a popularized result of his work. They created a mood which generated suspicion against any kind of dogmatism. Human knowledge is phenomenology, nothing more. Absolute judgments became suspect. Judgments could be offered only with the disclaimer, "or so it appears to me".[33]

One far reaching effect of this limitation of knowledge to phenomena is that the whole of life can no longer be brought under the rule of truth. In a sense, limiting reason to appearances is a gain over the older rationalism, because it left room for the acknowledgement that human beings are constituted by more than just the capacity to reason. There is a new awareness that feelings, and drives and the will must be reckoned as vital parts of human make-up. The problem, however, is that since knowledge is limited to what reason can know, and reason is limited to appearances, that which lies outside of the phenomenal realm cannot be judged by the question of truth. While Kant himself was confident that ethics could be rational, neo-Kantianism enshrined the dogma of limiting knowledge to the phenomenal realm while rejecting or ignoring his rational ethic. The result then, is that personal drives, or the power of the will, cannot be subordinated to an over-riding concern for truth. Thus the Kantian limits on reason divorced from a Kantian ethic leads directly the idea of the primacy of the unfettered will.[34]

In Schlatter's analysis, Kant altered the way the university and even the church asked the question of truth. While throughout the history of western thought the question of truth has been asked with great passion, after Kant the question of truth is displaced by the question of what is "reasonable" or what is "scientific". And as Schlatter rather mockingly states it, it was very easy for Kant a man of the university to determine what was "reasonable"; something is "reasonable" if it is found "in the lecture notes of a Wolffian".[35] For Schlatter, a healthy or rightly ordered thought process is one in which the knower is subordinate to that which is known. To know requires that one submit oneself to reality, be it the reality of nature or the reality of God. But a Kantian epistemology refuses that act of submission and chooses to first of all decide how it is that the thinking subject knows, and how reality must conform itself to the knowing subject. It begins by defining what is rationally possible for the subject to know, and then subordinates actuality to that prior definition of the possible.

The consequences of this emphasis on the priority of the rational synthesizing activity of the knower (though in actuality Kant does not speak of an empirical knower, but only of "reason") has far reaching consequences for our knowledge of God. When Kant turns to the question of our knowledge of God, he of course equates "knowledge" with "pure reason". And "in the lecture notes of a Wolffian", there are three possible rational ways of establishing the truth of God's existence.[36] This, according to

Schlatter, is Kant's great mistake. He assumes correctly that there must be a reason for belief in God, but errors in his assumption that the only possible valid source of that belief must be pure reason. It never occurs to him to actually investigate an empirical person like Paul or Augustine and ask how their certainty of the reality of God arose. Kant already knows *how* things are known, now he only needs to apply that knowledge to the question of our knowledge of God. Kant's analysis shows how it is that reason gives rise to the idea of God thus supposedly explaining why people hold that belief, but at the same time his critique of pure reason shows that the proofs go beyond the powers of reason and are thus inconclusive.

Schlatter believes that Kant's analysis of the question of God, raises the most fundamental theological question; namely that of how certainty of God (*Gewißheit Gottes*) arises. But at the same time his analysis undermines that certainty and leaves us incapable of resolving the issue. The problem is not simply that he undermines the classic rational proofs for the existence of God, it is that his entire epistemology is deaf to the ways in which God actually *does* work to implant faith within us. Schlatter does take issue with Kant's critique of the proofs; especially his argument that the idea of causality can only be used to link appearances.[37] But the real damage done by Kant is that the means which God in actuality uses to create faith are declared by him to be outside the bounds of possible knowledge. God, in Schlatter's understanding, bears witness to himself and awakens our certainty of him through the means of nature, history, and experience.[38] But in Kantian epistemology we no longer observe nature, nor are our lives situated in nature; nature is simply a mute parade of phenomena organized into a spatial-temporal order by the activity of our minds. History, like nature, is only a catalogue of phenomena which we organize within the limits of our idea of causation; an idea that cannot extend to address the question of how God can be creative of history. Experience occurs within our inner lives, and the self and its experiences are non-phenomenal. So experience, too, is ultimately unintelligible and unable to produce knowledge.

Kant is left then without rational certainty of God, but only a "postulate" of God's existence. As Schlatter characterizes it, Kant is left with a
"wish" for God; a feeble remnant of the traditional view of God which is
still useful because it fills certain purposes.[39] The process of knowing stems
entirely from our own activity. Reason creates our image of nature; it
creates the moral law, and through the activity of our own freedom we
fulfill that law. But one thing remains outside of our power; the power to
bring about the convergence of virtue and happiness. Since it is reasonable
to hope for the ultimate union of duty and happiness, it is reasonable to hope
for a power that is capable of producing that union.

As was mentioned earlier (p. 23–24), for Schlatter every epistemological question is at root a theo-relational matter. Kant's procedure
whereby a rational theory of subject-centered rational activity is made the
basis and presupposition of all knowledge, and knowledge is limited to that
which can be exhaustively comprehended by that activity, is not only bad
epistemology, it is a struggle against that which is given to us by God. In
a Kantian framework a rational theory of knowledge is needed so that we
can know what it *means* to know so that we *can* know. Schlatter sees the
pretentiousness of this approach as practically absurd. In the first section of
his *Briefe über Das Christliche Dogma*, Schlatter makes his point with a
reductio ad absurdum argument. He suggests that if we need a theory of
knowledge before we can know, then we would also need a theory of feeling
before we could feel and an understanding of the will before we could
will.[40] Knowledge and experience constantly present us with actualities
which must be affirmed even while they are mysterious and we do not know
how it is that they take place. For example:

> The question of how communication takes place between us human
> beings, and how the experience of another person enters into our
> perception, places us once again before an impenetrable mystery. But what
> historian gives up on his work because he does not know how something
> from the past can enter our consciousness?[41]

It is this obsession with a rational theory of knowledge as a pre-requisite to any knowledge that brings Schlatter's scorn against Kant as a destroyer of both knowledge and faith:

> It is on this ground, and this ground alone that I regard our Kantian theologians to be dangerous destroyers of science and the church. They have many corpses on their conscience, because their proposition that the theory of knowledge has a priority that conditions all further knowledge, produces the result that the life-act is damaged at its root. We would need a large clinic if we were to assemble all those even from only Württemberg whose capacity to think, to will, and to believe had been deeply incapacitated through their theory of knowledge.[42]

Against "Atheistic Methods"

While Schlatter attacks the effects of Kantian scepticism on ethics and our understanding of God, it is with its effects on the historical study of scripture that he most often occupies himself. It is the dogmatic use of the canons of Kantian scepticism that have made the scientific study of Scripture "Godless", and made scholarship blind to the reality of the creative work of God in history. Schlatter develops his criticism of Kantian scepticism in biblical studies in his discussion and evaluation of the "history of religions school" that had come to dominate biblical scholarship in the course of his lifetime. He characterizes and presents his basic criticism of this approach in his essay in *Die Religionswissenschaft der Gegenwart im Selbstdarstellungen*. Here, in a discussion of the goals and problems that have occupied him throughout his academic career, Schlatter characterizes his own work as being that of a "scientific worker" in the field of *Religionsgeschichte*.[43] But he very quickly parts company with the usual practitioners of the scientific study of the history of religion.

Schlatter states that he studies history because he wants to show how religious faith arises out of a particular history.[44] The object of his study is not historical events or documents in and of themselves. Since he is a Christian the object of his interest is to clarify how Christian faith is the product and the creator of a distinctive history. But this approach sets him at odds with the history of religions school.

> Essential to them (the history of religions school) is the conviction that religion has its essence in something other than history, something individual which does not need the community in order for it to arise, something timeless which is not subject to becoming, an idea or a feeling that is grounded in the suprahistorical essence of humanity.[45]

For Schlatter this dualism is one of the destructive consequences of rationalism. Wherever "greek logic" prevails that which is historical and individual comes under attack. That which is historical and individual belongs to that which is "accidental, contingent, past, that which veils the idea, the bark on the tree, the husk around the kernel, etc."[46] For the history of religions approach then, the New Testament becomes understandable when the historian shows how the history presented there is a contingent product of its time and place, and by this means the ahistorical and timeless "essence of religion" can be discovered and set free from its historical "husk". This dualism between religion and history means for the history of religions school that history is an object to be studied and explained within the limits of a Kantian phenomenology. Thus one studies history not to establish and ground a specific faith, but to discredit that history by showing that it is *not* essential to religion. In Schlatter's view then, any approach guided by this dualism will inevitably lead to polemics against the history of religion.

> Therefore the presentation of the history of religion inevitably becomes polemics against it. History ceases to be God's revelation, because from this standpoint, when religion is tied into history it becomes confused and corrupted.[47]

This basic critique of the history of religion's dualism between history and religion gets sharpened up and considerably expanded in Schlatter's essay, "Atheistiche Methoden in der Theologie".[48] This essay was written as a review and refutation of an article written by Paul Jäger in *Der Christlichen Welt* (1905, No. 25). In this article Jäger has sought to clarify the task of theology. In response to a claim by Wilhelm Lütgert (a friend of Schlatter) to the effect that biblical scholarship cannot ignore God, Jäger wants to present the counter-assertion that theology must use "atheistic methods".[49] Lütgert had summed up his position in the pregnant assertion that, "In every method lurks a dogmatic position".[50] Jäger insists on "atheistic methods" because they are by common consent the only strictly scientific methods. He declares his program by asserting:

> We want to explain the world (including religion both in its social development and in the experience of the individual) from the world...(that means)...we want to explain it via the powers that are a part of the world-process, without recourse to the idea of God.[51]

This is necessary because, Jäger argues, "the scientific method *ignorat deum*, it knows nothing of him". Jäger's argument is of course that this is the only way to truly be scientific.

This exclusion of God from the explanation of history should not distress the believer, according to Jäger, because it is only as a scientist that he ignores God. It is only in his scientific function that the theologian is ignorant of God. As a religious individual, however, the idea of God still continues to be in effect. Having excluded God from the scientific attempt to understand history, God can nevertheless still be known and claimed as a reality by the religious individual. Jäger is quite clear on his insistence that the scientific study of history of religion is something quite separate from the religious subjectivity of the individual. He attempts to clarify the distinction by suggesting that:

> Since science does not know God, therefore both the science of religion and scientific theology in the general history of religions as well as in biblical and church history should deal only with the subjective attitude of the individual.[52]

Schlatter's rejection of this thesis is sharp and caustic:

> This is the old sharply drawn dualism that we have come to know from Kant, Jacobi, Schleiermacher, Fries, etc.: The heathen head and the pious heart, atheistic science and religious feelings, etc.[53]

Schlatter's criticism of Jäger's thesis are many and complex. We will attempt to sort out the basic ones. His first criticism is that there simply is no basis on which to assert that science must ignore God. Schlatter is of the opinion that there are rules which must guide the scientific endeavor, but in his view those rules cannot be found or established in the spirit of the age, they can only arise because they are basic to our ability to know. There is but one clearly given universal law that applies to all scientific endeavor and that is:

> ...that before all judgments must stand observations, and before any of our own productions must stand the receptive act or else we fall into wind and illusions. An atheistic world-view is not a constitutive category of our capacity to know.[54]

The only rule that Schlatter will recognize as essential to science is the phrase from this essay that is often quoted of him, "Science is first seeing, and second seeing, and third seeing and ever and ever again seeing".[55]

Schlatter goes on to show that Jäger himself has nothing to base his insistence on atheistic methods on except his assertion that that is what he wants to do, and his observation that this is the generally accepted definition of scientific method. Jäger states the basis of his program by saying:

> We want (*wollen*) to have a scientific theology, that means a science of the religious life that stands in exact harmony with the scientific mentality and work of our time. We want to remain in contact with that which is regarded overall today as science...(Atheistic method) is the foundational scientific idea of our time.[56]

Schlatter takes some delight in pointing out the prominence Jäger gives to the *will* to be scientific. The decision to ignore God in historical methodology is in fact a decision, not something fundamentally based in science itself. While the essence of science, for Jäger, is thought, the very basis of his support for "atheistic method" shows that thought and will are never totally separable.

Schlatter also challenges the idea that Jäger is adequately describing modern scientific method. The "absolute rationality and clarifiability of nature" was an ideal found in the Cartesian and Spinozist worldview.[57] But, Schlatter asks, does the modern natural scientist or historian necessarily share this ultimate confidence that everything can be irreducibly comprehended in a mechanical model? Certainly all science is committed to observing and comprehending causal relationships to the furthest extent that that is possible. But this does not entail the necessity of a scientific method that ignores the question of deity. Jäger's method then, is not rooted in actual observation or in actual scientific work, but in the speculative assertion of an atheistic worldview

> The world-view that Jäger operates with—that is the idea that the world is a self explanatory unity, does not grow out of the observing of nature, or even less from the observation of history, but rather has speculative roots...Jäger rejects Lütgert's proposition: "In every historical method lurks a dogmatic system", but at the same time he is the perfect illustra-tion of its truth. His world-concept, that the world is a self-contained atheistic entity so that in all possible events nothing may or can become visible except the world itself, is itself a dogmatic position. Furthermore, it is a worthless dogmatic position because it has not been grounded or researched, but has simply been brought in as a law because that is supposedly the way "everyone" thinks. "The current age thinks this way, therefore we must think this way" is indeed a novel theological method; up until now the church never spoke that way.[58]

For Schlatter theology does not need to go "begging and borrowing" for a generally acceptable method.[59] Theology turns its eye toward the study of specific events which have given rise to faith. Theology's task is to observe these events and to explain how they are creative of faith, and it can only pursue this task if the theologian's eye is not diverted by hidden dogmas smuggled in as part of the theologian's method. "Atheistic method" and an "atheistic theology" are difficult to establish as true, indeed, they must be incorporated into theology as a dogma. However, an atheistic method or theology are quite vulnerable to challenge and even to disproof:

> Were it the case that the natural scientist never had any incentive to form the concept of God; were it the case that the historian never came across events that reached beyond the merely human; or never came across a law that is greater than the human will, or a law that the human will sinfully breaks; were it the case that even in the area that the theologian observes we never saw a well-founded basis for our awareness of God, let us say, *except* in the way in which Jesus lived his life in God, and that here in this one case we come upon an undeniable reality that compels our consent through its creative power; indeed the basis and content of our

theology would be small, but atheistic theology would be utterly destroyed.[60]

Having asserted that "atheistic method" is without scientific merit, Schlatter also goes on to point out what he feels is a basic internal contradiction in Jäger's position. While as a historian Jäger seems to be passionately committed to truth and adheres to an "atheistic method" since it is essential for the scientific explanation of historical phenomena, as a religious individual he is no longer under the power of this truth ideal. Having studied and explained the phenomena, Jäger suddenly starts to speak of "a higher voice".[61] It is as if after the theologian had explained religious phenomena atheistically he were suddenly to say, "I have now explained the appearances; now you may think what you want about the essence".[62] After having given "atheistic method" sovereignty over all knowledge the theologian suddenly sweeps all that knowledge aside and leaves the truth question up to the subjectivity of the religious individual. Science, which has been introduced to carry out the rule of truth seeking subjects everything to scepticism with the end result that the individual is no longer under the rule of truth but may make of the phenomena what they want.

In other words, Schlatter is saying that Jäger is not deeply enough committed to the truth. At least when it comes to the religious life of the individual science is forgotten and regarded as only preliminary work. Schlatter's pointed comeback to this is, *"True science does not exist in order to be forgotten"*(Schlatter's emphasis).[63]

Jäger is confident that after he has used his "atheistic method" to study religious phenomena he will still retain a basis on which as a religious individual he can still be religious. But, Schlatter observes, the basis for this confidence is mysterious. Whence comes the "higher knowledge" of the religious individual? To what extent are religious beliefs or feelings still under the rule of truth? Throughout the church's history the believer was under a claim to truth that came from the scriptures and previous generations. But for Jäger the New Testament needs to be explained without recourse to God, and the wisdom of past generations is "unscientific". So none of these authorities from the past can establish any claim to truth over the individual.

In short, for Schlatter the entire theological task has been subverted by Jäger's method. Theology's task is to show how our own faith and life arises out of the history and experiences of the past. Theology's goal is to build a community of faith that is bound by the reality and authority of these past events. Jäger's understanding of religion as the free subjective activity of the individual is possible only because he has failed to observe; he has failed to observe "that we with our own religiosity are part of a larger common life that binds successive generations to one another".[64] Religion is not a reality that lies beyond the truth question somewhere in the subjectivity of the individual, the faith of the Christian community arises out of a history in which God has been and is still active. A historical science that wills to be "atheistic" renders asunder the community's connection to its life-line and thus corrupts its relationship to God.

It should be pointed out here that Schlatter does not place all of the blame for this on Jäger or the larger history of religions school. One important comment in "Atheistische Methoden in der Theologie", suggests that the rip between religion and science, or between religion and history which has been accomplished by post-Kantian scholars was prepared already by tendencies in Protestant theology. Speaking of the gap between historical knowledge and individual religion Schlatter writes, "If one looks into the overall inner make-up of Protestantism it is not entirely surprising that Jäger can so easily complete this rending asunder."[65] This inner connection between Schlatter's criticism of Luther and his criticism of post-Kantian historical methodology will be the themes of Ch. VIII where I seek to fully establish my central thesis in this work.

Endnotes

1.*Die Religionswissenschaft der Gegenwart im Selbstdarstellungen*, ed. D. Erich Stange (Leipzig: Felix Meiner Verlag, 1925), 153.

2.Schlatter's extensive discussion of human awareness of God can be found in his extended essay entitled *Die Gründe der christlichen Gewißheit* (Stuttgart: Calwer Verlag, 1917).

3.*Rückblick auf meine Lebensarbeit*, 41.
   Die Philosophische Arbeit seit Cartesius, 25.

4.*Briefe über Das Christliche Dogma*, 17.

5.See my "A Biographical Introduction," pp. 3-4.

6.*Rückblick auf meine Lebensarbeit*, 33.

7.This extended essay was first released in the *Beiträge* in 1906, and was last issued by Calwer Verlag in 1959 under the title, *Die philosophische Arbeit seit Cartesius*, with a foreword by Helmut Thielicke.

8.*Rückblick auf meine Lebensarbeit*, 161.

9.*Briefe über Das Christliche Dogma*, 18-19.

10.*Die Gründe der christlichen Gewißheit*, 40.

11.Ibid., 19.

12.We will deal further with Schlatter's anthropology and its role in his theological method in chapter VII.

13.*Das Christliche Dogma*, 364-365. See the english translation of this chapter from Schlatter's dogmatics in my "Appendix A" following, especially pp. 169-172.

14.*Die Philosophische Arbeit seit Cartesius*, 28f.

15.Ibid., 30.

16.Ibid., 30,31.

17.Ibid.

18.While Schlatter does not go so far as to defend the role of "prejudice", he does want to establish a positive epistemological role for a thinker's life-story (*Lebensgeschichte*). While he too searches for objectivity, he rejects the idea that it is found by freeing oneself from the vast store of experiences and knowledge that are mediated to us through history and human community. Schlatter's point here sounds similar to Gadamer's attempt to show the positive role of "prejudice" in the appropriation of the past. (See

Gadamer's *Truth and Method*, pp. 238–253) Schlatter, though, is making a more modest point than Gadamer. Schlatter wishes only to show that the elimination of "prejudice" should not be the primary epistemological ideal of the interpreter.

19.Ibid., 36. Schlatter argues at one point that the ideal of thinking without prejudices would actually undercut our motive to learn. He argues that the ongoing awareness of the fragmentary nature of our knowledge and our awareness that our intellects are in many ways defective are powerful motives for further intellectual work.

20.Ibid., 32.

21.Ibid., 33.

22.Ibid., 34.

23.Ibid., 35.

24.Ibid., 40.

25.Ibid., 41.

26.Ibid., 43.

27.Ibid., 45.

28.*Briefe über Das Christliche Dogma*, 13-14.

29.*Die philosophische Arbeit seit Cartesius*, 107.

30.Ibid., 108.

31.Ibid., 109.

32.Ibid., 111.

33.Ibid., 112.

34.Ibid., 115.

35.Ibid., 119.

36.Ibid., 120-124, for Schlatter's discussion of Kant's treatment of the three classic rational "proofs" for the existence of God.

37.Ibid., 121-122.

38.See our discussion in Ch. VII, pp. 136ff.

39.Ibid., 125.

40.*Briefe über Das Christliche Dogma*, 10.

41.Ibid., 10.

42.Ibid., 10.

43.*Die Religionswissenschaft der Gegenwart im Selbstdarstellungen*, ed. D. Erich Stange (Leipzig: Felix Meiner Verlag, 1925), 161.

44.Ibid., 161.

45.Ibid., 161-162.

46.Ibid., 162. For Schlatter's criticism of Harnack in the same vein, see *Erlebtes*, p.85.

47.Ibid., 164.

48."Atheistichen Methoden in der Theologie", *Beiträge zur Förderung der christlicher Theologie* 9, 230ff.

49.Ibid., 230.

50.Ibid., 239.

51.Ibid., 231. The quote is from the Jäger article as quoted directly by Schlatter.

52.Ibid., 232.

53.Ibid., 241.

54.Ibid.

55.Ibid., 240.

56.Ibid., 239. (Jäger as quoted by Schlatter)

57.Ibid., 243.

58.Ibid., 240. This discussion dating from 1905 tends to suggest that the kind of program outlined by someone like Gordon Kauffman in his *Essay in Theological Method*, (Missoula, Mont: Scholar's Press, 1975), is not really all that innovative. Kauffman, like Jäger wants to insist that theology can affirm nothing that cannot be brought before the commonly accepted "bar of reason", which by general consensus ignores divine causality.

59.Ibid., 241.

60.Ibid.

61.Ibid., 245.

62.Ibid.

63. Ibid., 237.

64. Ibid.

65. Ibid., p. 238.

Chapter VI

HISTORY AND HISTORICAL UNDERSTANDING

The preceding chapter should have made it abundantly clear that Schlatter sets himself against any rational or *ir*rational flight from history. At a methodological level Schlatter's work must be seen as an attempt to consistently carry out a completely historicized understanding of human understanding and to apply that historicization even to the understanding of God and faith.[1] Having described his criticism of an ahistorical rationalism, it now seems appropriate to attempt to describe as well what Schlatter means by history and just how human understanding takes place within history. But here we come up against a fairly formidable obstacle. Schlatter does not have a general, theoretical definition of history. Indeed a theory of history that could be proposed or explicated before one had actually *observed* reality would contradict Schlatter's program. We can only begin by seeing or observing the particulars of what is. Only after having carefully observed can we begin to make judgments about the nature of history and human understanding in history.

For Schlatter the Christian believer, the history he observes will not be history in general. As a person who carries within himself a faith certainty (*Gewißheit Gottes*) that decisively shapes his thought and will he is bound to observe the specific history of which this certainty is a product. As a believer he will observe and reflect on the history that has given him his identity. Furthermore, Schlatter carries out his vocation as a historian in the service of the church and its faith; so it is not history in general, but a specific divinely created history that draws his attention. This means that if we are to present Schlatter's view of history we would once again need to present the history of the Christ; something we at least attempted to sketch in Ch. IV. So our task in this chapter will be to reflectively construct the view of history and historical understanding that we can abstract from Schlatter's concrete and specific work in understanding this specific history.

Actually, to present Schlatter's view of history would require a two-pronged approach. We would need to begin with a portrayal of his personal history; or what he calls his *Lebensgeschichte*. We have no choice when we begin to observe but to observe that which is available to us in our own consciousness.[2] But the believer finds within their own personal history an overriding reality that claims their attention, namely; faith. It becomes evident as one observes and reflects on faith that it does not arise out of the person's own self-consciousness, nor is it a product that they have synthesized and created through reflecting on intellectual abstractions. Rather it is overwhelmingly evident that faith has been planted in their personal history through their encounter with God in Christ. It becomes evident through observation that the believer's will and life has encountered and become obedient to another personal will and life, that of God in Christ. So while one necessarily begins with the consciousness of the believer, the nature of faith compels the Christian community to focus its attention *first* and *primarily* on the history of the Christ.

The Christian historian-theologian then has a very specific task and that is to observe the biblical history and to clarify how the active presence and creative grace of God is mediated to the Christian community through the history of the Christ. The Christian historian does not begin from some neutral, theoretical vantage point. Rather he or she is *already* in possession of a life determining faith and the historical task will be complete when it is shown just how faith has come to be in and through this particular history. The believing historian begins with the awareness that faith is a God-created *actuality* and is thus also a *possibility*.[3] The concern of the believing historian, then, is to clarify and strengthen faith by more clearly illuminating how God is creatively active in Jesus.

So Schlatter begins with a specific history; both his own personal history of faith, and the biblical history of Christ. He will go beyond those specific histories, however, to claim that these histories are paradigmatic for all history and thus one can make generalizations about history and historical understanding based on the specific history of faith. In fact, it is in the relationship of the Christian community to its history that we can see what a properly or fruitfully ordered human life is. It is in the Christian community that we finally see how human life is meant to be lived in and from history, and what a normal approach to understanding and appropriating history is.

In keeping with these preliminary comments, the remainder of this chapter will fall into two sections in which we will present a reflective synthesis of Schlatter's understanding of historical events, and the kind of historical understanding that is appropriate, or corresponds fully to the reality of historical events.

The Problematics of Historical Events

For Schlatter history is a series of "small and even smaller" realities that the historian must carefully observe.[4] History presents us with an inexhaustibly rich and complex series of particulars. Furthermore, every historical reality is closely linked to its environment in an ever expanding circle of associations and relationships. While Schlatter's own historical observing is centered on the Christ of the New Testament, his work does not confine itself to the New Testament. He finds that in order to understand it he must understand the cultural and linguistic environment in which Jesus carried out his mission. So he turns his attention to Palestine and the synagogue. He also finds himself in an intellectual environment which has been shaped by the Reformation and by the intellectual heritage of rationalism. So in order to gain clear access to the New Testament he must observe the history of the church and the western philosophical heritage. This inter-relatedness of all history means that the task of the historian is endless. In fact we can never understand any historical event fully. The details and complex associations that make up each historical reality go far beyond any historian's power to see and comprehend. History also presents a unique challenge to our understanding because past events possess unique individuality. Nature is certainly just as complex as history and the natural sciences have certainly developed tools which do a masterful job of comprehending this complexity. But the task of historical science cannot simply borrow the procedures and assumptions of the natural sciences, primarily because the natural sciences do not study events that possess full individuality:

> Historical knowledge differentiates itself from the natural sciences by the fact that it deals with completely individualized events. Historical life places us before that which is concrete, it places us before a totally determinate life-act. Events have individuality in the fullest sense of the word. Even though individuation is not fully lacking in nature, we are being true to the subject matter of the natural sciences when we establish the priority of "the typical" and form schemata and rules which comprehend the processes of nature in all their wide reaching dimensions. In the attempt to understand historical events, however, "the typical", that is the quest for general historical laws, must retreat.[5]

The natural sciences have been successful through following a method which demands that all the phenomena investigated conform to a set of rules. The assumption that nature is law-like and rationally penetrable has produced remarkably productive results, therefore that assumption is well-founded and valid. Schlatter sees much of 19th century historiography as the attempt to transfer the same assumptions to the study of history. History too was to be made intelligible and comprehensible by bringing all events into the framework of a law-like causality which can lay bare the origin of the event.[6] But the irony is that the failure to distinguish the unique character of historical as opposed to natural phenomena leads to the destruction of the historian's ability to see and comprehend.

Perhaps another way to address the question of the uniqueness of history as opposed to nature, is to say that historical events while they are publicly observable the way natural events are, also originate in the inner life of human (and divine) agents. Therefore, historical events cannot simply be comprehended by analogy to natural events. Historical events have an "inner" dimension. That is, they arise out of a personal life-act, and again, the personal cannot be irreducibly comprehended under a schemata of causal laws as can natural phenomenon. The mysterious elements of personal life lie hidden from our immediate view, and since historical events have a personal quality they cannot be comprehended within a rigid schemata of law-like causality. The historian cannot be an "objective" observer, unless they honor the individuality and personal qualities of the event they are observing.

Furthermore, most historical events lie hidden in forgetfulness. History is not only memory, it is also forgetting. Much that is needed to fully understand the past is lost to us forever. As Schlatter states it, "As important as memory is, the function of forgetting is just as important in the household of our personal life."[7] Forgetting is important to us because without it the past in all its fullness would be immediately present to us and would virtually eliminate the possibility for us to develop our own God-given potential and to exercise our creative freedom.

But this means then that, "All-knowing-ness is here denied to us"...[8] History denies us that which the rationalist pursues as the goal of all knowing; absolute intellectual certainty. But to Schlatter this relinquishment of the ideal of perfect knowledge is in keeping with what we observe in human experience and is congruent with our status as creatures. Rationalism is finally a sinful attempt to leap out of the limits that are set for us as part of our creatureliness.

Not only are historical events impossible to fully comprehend because they are complex and surrounded by much which is forgotten; the events of the New Testament elude complete comprehension because their ultimate source lies hidden in the creative work of God. Here we encounter what could appear to be a paradox in Schlatter's thought. We have noted already that Schlatter believes that the historian must pursue the question of causality, and that even the question of divine causality is not a question the historian can ignore. But the other side of this is that Schlatter also recognizes and honors the mystery of God's creative work.

While Schlatter affirms that faith comes to be out of the work of God in history, and that our faith is grounded in the particulars of historical reality, he realizes that we never immediately or objectively see the hand of God in history. While we need to observe and explain faith as the fruit of the work of God in history:

> That does not mean that we must lay bare without remainder the coming to be of faith from its ultimate causes. To make such a claim would be to throw ourselves against the inescapable boundaries of our consciousness. Our eye never lays hold of beginnings; never do we look upon the ultimate causal powers as they go about their work. It is always the results of their work which first offer themselves to our perception. . . There is no theory of creation which could make the creation of faith comprehensible. We have done our complete duty in the realm of knowing when we correctly perceive that what stands before us in the illuminated realm of our consciousness stands before us as the product of that realm of becoming which is permanently hidden from us.[9]

Or we could cite this somewhat simpler and more eloquent testimony:

> We can only ever observe the results of the life creating processes, and never do we enter the workshop in which the finger of God creates life and faith.[10]

So Schlatter's claim that the historian must press the question of causality even back to the question of divine causation, is not a naive claim that the hand of God can be objectively laid hold of. The history which he seeks to observe is in fact rooted in a creative mystery which lies far beyond the range of our vision. Yet the results of that creative and mysterious work *do* lie before us "in the illuminated realm of our consciousness" and by virtue of being there must provoke us to seek after a full understanding of their origins. But a full understanding "of what stands before us" does not mean that we must thoroughly penetrate reality with an act of reason. In fact, the fact that we cannot ultimately penetrate the mysterious is simply another reminder that we are creatures, and we are not our own lords. For

Schlatter this ineradicable realization of our creatureliness is one of the pre-conditions which makes our knowledge of God possible. By honoring the limits of our ability to see and understand, we in fact, make true seeing and understanding possible.

> Because we are not the creator we also cannot see or grasp any creative act. At the point where our calling ends our seeing and understanding also ends. The limitation that is thereby given to our consciousness is a clear witness to the fact that we are not our own creation, and are also not our own lords. Our unovercomeable incapacity for our sight to reach to ultimate beginnings is the sign that we are created and ruled over. If we make the claim that we are all-knowing then we put ourselves into a struggle with the inner law that forms us.[11]

The Possibility of Historical Mediation

But the immensity of history and the virtual impossibility of complete understanding in no way leads Schlatter toward pessimism. Rather he sees the complexity of history as a challenge and a summons to lovingly and patiently observe and thus clarify a wide range of historical relationships. The limitations that history imposes on our understanding has given rise to the mistaken assumption that ultimate, religious convictions cannot possibly be grounded in historical events and judgments. But this dissatisfaction with "mere" historical knowledge is, in his view, the result of a misguided intellectual perfectionism. The perfectionism which originates in Socrates and Plato, and finds renewed expression in Descartes and through him found its way into the natural sciences is a false and destructive intellectual goal when applied to history, and when applied to faith. Schlatter is quick to acknowledge that, "None of our ideas are completely correct".[12] Perfectionism is false because it denies our creaturely limits, and because it inevitably leads to skepticism. Finally when we come to see that perfect understanding is denied us then we retreat into a skepticism which claims that since perfect knowledge is denied us, we can know nothing, at least nothing that really matters, with utter certainty. Speaking of human understanding, Schlatter writes:

We have suffered great damage because of our distress regarding that
which we lack, because this has tempted us to struggle against the natural
conditions of our life; conditions which are givens (*die uns gesetzt sind*).[13]

Having conceded the ideal of penetrating history and uncovering the
ultimate causal laws that determine it; having surrendered the ideal of
rational completion in historical understanding; Schlatter more or less
triumphantly notes we have finally lost nothing except perhaps the confusion
produced by a debilitating ideal.

Schlatter approaches history with confidence. For him the question
is not whether we can perfectly comprehend history, or accurately
reconstruct what has happened in the past. He is perfectly willing to stop
where the historical sources do:

The fact that limitations are set to our observations by the meager extent
of the sources, and that these cannot be overcome, must not lead us to fill
in the gaps with romancing constructions. The glory of academic work is
not that it knows everything, but that it sees what the witnesses make
visible and is silent where they are silent.[14]

The question then for Schlatter is not whether we can know the past
perfectly, rather it is whether or not history has sunken effect-less into the
past and whether or not its vitalities are forever lost to us. And to him,
human experience, in particular the experience of faith, dramatically
demonstrates that history does not stand before us mute and unintelligible.
Rather human experience shows that history mediates to us a knowledge
which is capable of renewing and creating personal life. History is
understood, not when it is rationally comprehended, but when we come into
a fruitful and creative relationship with the *effects* that issue from historical
events. But now we need to inquire into the bases or grounds on which
Schlatter believes this historical mediation is possible. How is it possible for
the effects of historical events to continue to be creatively appropriated?

As has been noted before, for Schlatter the historian's task is to
"observe" what is there, and it is not his or her task to construct what is *not*
there. To him a good deal of modern historical scholarship is of no value
whatsoever because it sees its task as that of reconstructing the past through

hypothetical constructions of the sequence and causal connections of past events. Moreover, these hypothetical reconstructions are doubly worthless because they are guided by ungrounded reductionist assumptions about historical causality. Schlatter sets himself the task of observing what is there in the most straightforward, objective sense of the word; namely the language of the biblical texts. This attention to language is fundamental to the possibility of historical understanding and mediation.

The relationship between language and history is an area largely unexplored in Schlatter scholarship, and one could even add that though this relationship is clearly critical to his work, he himself does not fully explore this relationship theoretically. In perhaps his most straightforward affirmation of the relationship between history and language, Schlatter simply declares, "History is linguistics" (*Geschichte ist Sprachkunde*).[15]

Perhaps we can best begin to understand this straight-forward though enigmatic statement if we return to our discussion of Schlatter's career and to his biographical writings. Schlatter recounts that in his *Gymnasium* days it was philology, and especially the history of language that won his attention.[16] Through the study of Greek and Roman poets he reports that he had developed "an eye for the coming-to-be of language".[17] Even more than that, one could say that Schlatter developed a sense that language is how history finds expression, and that it is language that gives us the possibility of historical understanding. It was the study of language that trained his eye to observe and be attentive to the "small and even smaller" details of history. But it is extremely important to note that the details to which he attends are *not* the details of factual, empirical information about events. It is these empirical details that are largely hidden in forgetfulness; and these factual details themselves do not convey history as personal life to us. The facts themselves stand before us fairly mute. The historical details that Schlatter *does* attend to are *linguistic* details.

Schlatter makes clear his preference for language over historical details in a discussion of the nature of New Testament history in his essay,

"The Theology of the New Testament and Dogmatics". Here he makes it clear that our access to history is through the biblical texts. And he shows that the biblical texts are not merely the means with which to reconstruct historical events:

> This is why the knowledge granted to the apostles is more important than the events. It is the permanent result of the history, whereas the history itself is largely forgotten and lost without trace. Their word, on the other hand, cuts loose from the turn of events and becomes a permanent power. It is this intellectual result of the course of history with which we are in the first place engaged, because this is responsible for the continuing effect of the New Testament. For the means whereby the New Testament history grasps and moves our own history is through the word which has come from it.[18]

It is this attention to language that Schlatter himself regards as critical to his ability to overcome the dominant 19th century dichotomy between history and faith; or between contingent, particular events and universal truths. If one attends primarily to the question of ordering histori-cal phenomena in a space-time manifold, and then subsequently asks how noumenal causation or religious truth is related to these particular phenome-na, one does admittedly end up with Lessing's "ugly ditch". But Schlatter regards his focus on language as a way to avoid setting up the problem of the "ugly ditch" to begin with. In describing his early approach to historical study Schlatter reports that for him, ..."the preoccupation with the singular and small and the elevation (of my attention) to the full-blown supernatural, the patient attention to concrete details and the sweeping flight to God are all inseparable."[19] He reports that he saw no conflict or gap between his asking the question of God, and giving his attention fully to the details of the world. This unified vision was later challenged when he discovered historical critical reflection; but throughout his career he maintained this unified view of faith and history:

> Along with the look which seeks to penetrate into the world I also turned toward that which is above. And along with the attention I focused on that which is above, I sought to see the world, even its smallest detail. If this could succeed, or whether or not this was possible did not bother me at all in my youth. Critical reflection on the theory of knowledge entered

into my life-act much later. But when I did address these questions my answers took the form that was already determined in my early education. *Because I came to be a theologian through the guidance of a linguist, I never had a theology that forgot history, or a history that hid God from my view* (emphasis mine) .[20]

That Schlatter studied history from the vantage point of a linguist is not merely something that colors his methods and perceptions, it is essential to his attempt to heal that which Kant had torn asunder. With Kant, you could say that Schlatter attends to phenomenal reality. But it is not the kind of phenomenal reality which consists of data that needs to be ordered in a time-space sequence. Since the phenomenal data that Schlatter attends to is *language* that means he does not begin with phenomenal data considered apart from noumenal realities; rather he begins with phenomenal data that also communicates "noumenal" claims. Language is a fully historical phenomenon which is completely inseparable from the contingencies of its time and place. But it is Schlatter's experience and his insistence that attending to this contingent, time-bound reality brings one face-to-face with the claim and the reality of divine presence and activity.

Schlatter then refuses to phenomenologically "bracket out" the divine agency claims that are mediated to us by biblical language. He refuses to accept Kant's claim that we are rationally incompetent to judge the truth of divine agency claims, and in fact he believes that in carefully and fully attending to the claims mediated through the language of scripture the causal connections which evidence the hand of God in human experience can be laid bare. If we attempt as historians to carefully observe the inner logic of the language in which the New Testament makes its claims, we will in fact find that those claims are only intelligible if they are grounded in the causal work of a divine agent. We never see "the finger of God" in history, but we do find claims about Christ, and the effect of Christ in the life of the disciple community, that cannot be rendered intelligible in any other way than to claim that it is the work of God.

This emphasis on language as a mediator of historical realities does not, however, stand by itself. There is no evidence that language has some kind of quasi-mystical status, or that Schlatter has in mind some independent ontology of language. Language is an expression of personal life. To be intelligible language needs to be interpreted as the expression of a community's experience, and as a testimony to the realities which have laid hold of and formed the history of a distinctive expression of the "life-act". Language is the medium through which the effects of history come to us, but history itself *is* human community. Ultimately history is mediated to us through the community which *is* the effect that God's work in history creates and sustains.

Language and community are closely related because it is language that gives us the possibility of thought, and language is not our private possession, but is a product of a common life. Though it is thought which gives us our self-consciousness and the uniqueness of our own identity, it is never the isolated self that thinks:

> We cannot think without language and language is not our private property but is the inherited possession of the community. We become able to speak, and therefore to think, through those who speak to us. That which we receive is the presupposition of anything which we ourselves produce...[21]

Our capacity to understand and to know God is not lodged somewhere deep within our own individuality but rather, "mediates itself to us through our association with those who share life with us."[22]

This relationship between history and community appears consistently in Schlatter's work. Perhaps it is stated most clearly in the following quote which indicates the relationship between history, community and language as that is focused in the scriptures:

> Therefore God *creates* history; history as the mutually conditioned life and relationships that are joined together to form a community; history as the joining of life into a chain of tradition which continues to form subsequent life. This does not entail a belittling of the work and power of the Spirit, but is precisely that which the Spirit wills and works. For that reason, the effective power of the scriptures consists in how they emerge out of history and how they continue to create history. Scripture creates history

in that it brings to our thought and will the reality of what happened in the past so that our present life receives its form and content from it.[23]

An exposition of the preceding quote would go far in explaining the entirety of Schlatter's method and theology. What the creative grace of God creates is not merely doctrines for the mind, or feelings for the soul, or imperatives for the will. God creates a new history, and God's work is mediated to us as a history which is creative of our history. That with which we make contact in the New Testament is a community that expresses its new history in the language of the biblical witness. Schlatter believes that an approach to scripture which seeks to isolate doctrine which we can then affirm, or which seeks after the religious experiences of scripture which we can then also experience, or which seeks after the ethical content of scripture which can then obey, will be non-productive. None of these approaches bring us into real contact with history so none of them can in turn be creative of history:

> When we speak of history we must immediately appropriate the concept "community" and say that those who lived before us have made our lives possible, and that we have made possible the lives of those who are born from us. The community generates actual, effective causal relations.[24]

It is only the history lived and passed on by a human community that is capable of generating further understanding and appropriation of the past. It is only living, fully personal life in all the richness of its relationships that can provide the "actual, effective causal relations" that can generate subsequent life. Historical events understood in their law-like causal relationships to one another, or a set of ideas abstracted from history and explicated through their internal logic, cannot create life. They remain ungrounded and ineffectual. So history, and with it, community, is the medium through which the Spirit continues its creative role. The only effective causal relationship is that of full giving and receiving in a human community:

> Therefore it is history and only history which is capable of mediating faith to us, because history prepares for us the entirety of our inner heritage out of which we create when we bring our own free, personal life-act to fruition.[25]

To go back to the quote with which we began this discussion (p. 116), history is "the mutually conditioned life and relationships that are joined to form a community", or is "the joining of life into a chain of tradition which continues to form subsequent life." History is the experience, convictions and acts of a human community and it is this personal, lived and experienced history, that mediates itself to us by continuing to be creative of personal life. And as he also points out, this "does not entail a belittling of the work and power of the Spirit, but is precisely that which the Spirit wills and works." We will address this further in Ch. VIII, but here we see a statement of Schlatter's concept of the creativity of divine grace. The Spirit is not glorified by working over and above history in the life of the individual, rather the Spirit's greatness and graciousness consists in working in and through history to create history. Only by working through the medium of fully personal human life, can the Spirit *create* fully personal human life in the divine image. Any attempt to escape history is then an escape as well from the creative power of God and the "actual, effective causal relations" through which God works.

One can see then, that the greek heritage which separates the divine which is eternal and unchanging from the material world which is temporal and limited has tended to blind us to the actual creative work of God which is tied up entirely in the temporal realm of becoming and change. Our bias is that anything that bears the mark of historicity must be alienated from the divine.[26] For Schlatter, this alienation between Spirit and history is pre-Christian and has not yet taken into consideration the distinctive character of grace.

One would need to add as well then, that while historical understanding is mediated through language as an expression of a community's experience and outlook, Schlatter leaves open the question of exactly *how* this understanding takes place. The eye of the historian can see *that* it is mediated through these means, but the actual process of understanding and mediation is mysterious. In other words, while Spirit and history are not alienated, neither are they merged. Schlatter is still able to say that historical understanding is not simply mediated by immanent historical processes that can be exhaustively comprehended, but is in the final analysis the work of the Spirit. Schlatter's confidence in the possibility of historical mediation is finally a confessional confidence in the on-going work of the Spirit.

The Epistemology of "Observation"

For Schlatter it is not our ability to know, in and of itself, that makes historical understanding a possibility. In a sense, for him, it is history itself that is the active partner in the relationship. History *seeks* to make *itself* known. The epistemology which is congruent with this conviction is one of "observation" (*Wahrnehmung*, or sometimes, *Beobachtung*). We have already made numerous references to Schlatter's use of the concept of "observation".[27] What remains to do be done is to give more sustained reflection to this concept and to show more clearly its role in his thought.

"Observation" is the first and most fundamental element of what Schlatter calls the "thought-act" (*Denkakt*). Observation needs to precede and ground the second element of the thought-act which he calls "judgment" (*Urteil*). Yet, finally both "observation" and "judgment" are a part of one unified "thought-act" and neither can ever be fully separated from the other.[28]

Understanding must begin with observation because we ourselves are not creators. Rationalism must fail because it believes that we generate knowledge out of ourselves through our own capacity to form judgments. But we cannot think and form judgments without first receiving.[29] Observing is the first order of business, and our task at this stage is, "the ongoing clarification and expansion of our field of vision (*Sehfeld*)".[30]

This call to observe, however, is to be distinguished from mere empiricism. Empiricism holds that the receiver is passive and that the data

thus received is that which is strictly limited to the senses. Schlatter wants
to maintain that in the process of observing the person is keenly engaged
and exerts a strenuous effort, even though it is an effort to be receptive.
Observation and judgment can never be totally separated because it is a
person; that is, an already historically determinate life that is doing the
observing. Instead of just passively receiving, one could say that for
Schlatter, the act of observing involves a moral and even spiritual effort. In
the process of observing the observer's personhood is not negated; in fact
the form of their personal life is a factor (for better or worse) in their
observations. Observing requires our highest efforts and powers:

> The historian in his historical work can never deny or annihilate his own
> convictions, so that his observation and his judgments do not affect one
> another; nor should he. The attempt to make oneself into a life-less mirror
> that only attempts to grasp and pass on foreign life is always unsuccessful,
> and is both logically and ethically false.[31]

The success of our attempts at understanding depend entirely on the care
with which we observe that which lies before us and thus place it in our
consciousness as a given reality. If we form a priori or premature judgments
the whole process must fail. That does not mean that absolute objectivity is
attainable or even desirable. The observer is always motivated and guided
by personal interests and experience. But we can say that observing has
succeeded when we can be certain that what stands before us in our
consciousness is not something generated by our will, but something that has
genuinely been received by us as a given that stands outside us.

Since observation is not merely passive, that means that our judging
activity is never completely absent or inactive in the process of observation.
Without the capacity for judgment that which we see would be mute and
life-less. Our capacity to judge is a given of our personal life.[32] We can
only observe history if we seek to penetrate the subject-matter by asking
questions about the relationship of the subject-matter to its environment, and
the interconnections that make the subject-matter an intelligible, unified
whole. In order to observe we must not suppress questions about causality

and the unity of the whole. These questions originate in our own inner life and we would be denying ourselves, or perhaps more critically, we would be failing to *observe* our own personhood if we did not actively pursue those questions. But we can only pursue them faithfully if we allow the subject-matter to display and demonstrate its own inner causal relationships, or its own internal order. We dare not import any prior concept of causality.

We should also point out what was noted earlier (p. 109f.), that is, that for Schlatter the historian observes both the "outer" and the "inner" aspects of a historical event. In fact the outer event is primarily an invitation to explore its inner logic. This again distinguishes his "observing" from mere empiricism. There is clearly in Schlatter an empathetic, or even spiritual aspect to observing and penetrating to the inner dimensions of an event. This again means that the whole personhood of the observer is active in the process. This inner dimension of events is (as we have noted) available to us primarily in language. It is through language that the real historical causal connections, the real inner dynamic of the event, becomes visible. And these inner dynamics are not discovered through a life-less objectivity, but because our own inner life equips with us with activities and analogies which enable us to penetrate the inner dimensions of events and make judgments about them.

Judgment, then, is the process whereby we unite that which we have observed with that which already is a part of our own inner life and heritage.

> After the life process has placed something as a "given" in our consciousness (be it through an external or internal process), we subsequently determine through a process of judgment what relationship exists between that which is given to us, and our already existing intellectual heritage.[33]

Judgment is the process whereby we grasp that which we have observed conceptually, and then either reject it or affirm it. But the key point again, is that judgment itself cannot create truth. We observe experience; we observe actual historical realities; and it is these historical realities that give meaning and substance to our concepts. We don't bring truth to our experiences through the activity of reasoning, we bring content to our concepts through experience. But we are thinking beings so we must appropriate experience through judgments.

Objectivity does not consist then in a life-less empiricism, but rather in the care with which we observe how we have come to make our judgments.

> The rightness of our thought-act essentially rests on the degree of control with which we watch over the relationship that exists between the facts that have been observed by us to our already existing knowledge.[34]

Since in the process of judgment our own productive powers come into play more than they do in the process of observation, our intellectual integrity consists of observing our own judgment process and being clear on why we judge the way we do.

In the act of judgment, Schlatter says, we follow a law of unity that is rooted in our own inner life. We cannot stop the process of observing because it inevitably leads us to the question of how that which is observed ties into our picture of the whole. In observing we always must ask how each individual event fits into its larger environment, but finally we must also ask how it fits into the way we ourselves think and feel and act. If we do not complete that process we can only remain alienated from that which we have observed, and being alienated from it, having made no judgment regarding it, we cannot claim to understand it.

Historical observation leads us inevitably to a point of decision, and this is, of course, especially true of the New Testament which confronts with a claim about Jesus as the Christ. To say "yes" to that claim is to have faith. Faith is simply the carrying through of our observation of the New Testament to the point where we make a life-changing affirmation of the truth of its claim. And for Schlatter, the fact that a historian has made that affirmative judgment regarding the claims of the New Testament does not then illegitimately bias him or make her observations "unscientific". In fact, carrying through the thought-act of observing the New Testament to the point of making it a part of one's own life-act demonstrates what a normal and complete thought-act is. Ultimately, having carried the act of observing the New Testament to the point of making a believing judgment regarding its claims makes one better able to penetrate the logic and meaning of the New Testament, and to make that inner meaning apparent to others.

In conclusion, one could say that Schlatter's epistemology of "observation" is an attempt to acknowledge the knowing subject's active role in the process of understanding, but it is also an attempt to overcome Kant's idea that the knowing subject is sovereign in the act of knowing. His epistemology allows history to mediate itself to the contemporary knowing subject in a way which does not negate the activity of the subject, but which allows the real causal connections of the historical object to control the exchange.

Endnotes

1.One must be cautious in applying the concept of historicism to Schlatter. Generally that word has been used to describe precisely the kind of skeptical, reductionistic historical study that Schlatter rejects. But in fact Schlatter would regard himself as a more consistent historicist than the historians he criticizes. He is more consistent in that: 1) he does not import a priori categories of understanding into the study of history, and 2) he does not abandon a historical approach when he considers the question of religious truth. Therefore, I believe it is fair to describe him as at least attempting to be a *consistent* historicist.

   For another discussion of the epistemological and theological significance of Schlatter's understanding of history see Klaus Bockmühl's "Die Wahrnehmung der Geschichte in der Theologie Adolf Schlatters", in *Die Aktualität der Theologie Adolf Schlatters*, ed. Klaus Bockmühl (Giessen/Basel: Brunnen Verlag, 1988), pp. 93–112.

2.*Briefe über Das Christliche Dogma* (Stuttgart: Calwer Verlag, 2nd ed., 1978), 13–14. We will give sustained attention to Schlatter's understanding of the person in Ch. VII.

3.This is just the reverse of a post-Kantian skeptical approach which first rationally defines what it is *possible* for the human subject to know and then proceeds to cut actuality to fit their a priori definition of historical possibility.

4.*Die Religionswissenschaft im Selbstdarstellungen*, 163.

5.*"Der Glaube und die Geschichte", from a collection of essays entitled, *Gesunde Lehre* (Freizeit-Bücher Nr. 4, Freizeiten Verlag zu Delbert im Rheinland, 1929), 339–340.

6.This may be a good time to bring in Ernst Troeltsch's classic essay "On Historical and Dogmatic Methods". From Schlatter's perspective, Troeltsch's insistence on the comprehensiveness of "analogy" in historical investigation, is a method which establishes "the typical" prior to observing the actual. It is an attempt to gain for the historian the scientific control and thus the certainty that the natural sciences can claim. But to Schlatter it would be an "unscientific" method because it is not true to the individuality and personal quality of historical subject-matter.

7.*Das Christliche Dogma* (Stuttgart: Calwer Verlag, 1911), 83.

8.Ibid., 82.

9.*Die Gründe der christliche Gewißheit* (Stuttgart: Calwer Verlag, 1927), 33.

10."Der Glaube und die Geschichte", 347.

11.*Das Christliche Dogma*, 36.

12."Nature, Sünde und Gnade", from *Gesunde Lehre*, 54.

13.Ibid.

14. "The Theology of the New Testament and Dogmatics", 143.

15. "Glaube und Geschichte", 340.

16. *Rückblick auf meine Lebensarbeit* (Stuttgart: Calwer Verlag, 2nd. ed., 1977), 28–33. See our discussion in "A Biographical Introduction", p. 3–4, preceding.

17. Ibid., 32.

18. "The Theology of the New Testament and Dogmatics", 157.

19. *Rückblick auf meine Lebensarbeit*, 116.

20. Ibid., 33.

21. *Die Gründe der christlichen Gewißheit*, 82–83.

22. Ibid., 83.

23. *Das Christliche Dogma*, 368.

24. "Der Glaube und die Geschichte", 343.

25. Ibid.

26. Ibid., 345.

27. See Ch. II, pp. 21 (and endnote #7), preceding.

28. Schlatter explains the relationship of these two elements of thought in several locations. We will especially refer to his article "Die Bedeutung der Methode für die theologische Arbeit" from *Theologischer Literaturbericht*, No. 4, January, 1908, esp. pp. 6–7; and his chapter on "Wahrnehmung und Urteil", pp. 89–93 in *Das Christliche Dogma*. Another very significant discussion of "observation" is found in *Die Gründe der christlichen Gewißheit*, ch. 4, "Die Wahrheit", pp. 40–51.

29. *Das Christliche Dogma*, 89.

30. "Die Bedeutung der Methode für die theologische Arbeit", 6.

31. Ibid., 8.

32. We will give further attention to what Schlatter refers to as the "laws of thought" in our discussion of his anthropology in Ch. VII.

33. "Die Bedeutung der Methode für die theologische Arbeit", 6.

34. Ibid., 7.

Chapter VII

ANTHROPOLOGY AND THE TASK OF THEOLOGY

The nature of Schlatter's theological program is such that the various theological tasks are co-relative and interdependent. There is no starting point or formal *Prinzip* which must either rationally or fideistically be established as the basis from which all else must follow. The theological task neither formally nor substantially follows the paradigm of syllogistic deduction. Each aspect of the theological task has a relative priority and independence vis-a-vis the entire program. For Schlatter, the two horizons of the theological task, the historical and the dogmatic, are on the one hand functionally interdependent rather than autonomous endeavors; and yet on the other hand, each horizon has an integrity and function that dare not be collapsed into the other. It is the ignoring of the relative independence and functional interdependence of the two horizons of theology that has lead some interpreters of Schlatter to label him a "biblicist" on one hand, while other interpreters understand him to be a practitioner of a form of "*Bewußt-seinstheologie*". Both labels have some truth in them, and that being the case neither can be fully true in and of itself. Schlatter himself scoffed at both labels.[1]

Readers of Schlatter who know him primarily as the historian, as the observer and interpreter of the New Testament, may be mystified by Schlatter the dogmatic theologian. As a historian Schlatter insists that the actualities of the past be given a self-less, openly receptive treatment. This requires that our understanding of historical possibilities, and our understandings of historical method be set aside. Our understanding of "possibilities" must not be allowed to constrain "actualities". In short, our own self-understanding must not be imposed on the biblical text. The surprise comes then, when Schlatter the dogmatic theologian begins his *Das Christliche Dogma* with an extended treatment of anthropology under the revealing title of "Der Mensch Das Werk Gottes".[2] Indeed, fully one-half of his work on dogmatics is included under the rubric of "anthropology". Schlatter can even go so far as to say that theology must of necessity be "anthropocentric".[3]

The role and significance of this anthropological focus is critical to the understanding of the whole of Schlatter's work. It would be easy to regard Schlatter primarily as a New Testament scholar and commentator who only occasionally dabbled in dogmatics and whose dogmatic writings can therefore be ignored. But that very tendency leaves out of the picture Schlatter's own insistence that the historical task is not complete in itself, and leads to an inadequate understanding of his work precisely *as* a biblical commentator. Those interpreters who ignore *Das Christliche Dogma* are likely to see him as a simplistic biblicist, and those who do take it seriously are more likely to see him as a theologian of human self-consciousness. Since his work in dogmatics is so critical to understanding his theological method, and since his anthropology is so essential to his dogmatics, it is imperative that we come to some understanding of the role of anthropology within his method as a whole. The challenge here is to integrate Schlatter the "anthropocentric" theologian with Schlatter the historian whose only interest is self-less attention to the actualities of the biblical history. The integration of these two seemingly disparate approaches is multi-faceted, but in our final chapter we will show that their integration can be most fully comprehended under our thesis of the centrality of the creative God in Schlatter's theology.

Schlatter himself provides a framework for interpreting the role of anthropology in his theological method in his introductory section of *Das Christliche Dogma*. Under the heading of "The Object of Dogmatics", he both re-affirms his objectivist understanding of revelation, *and* explains why an anthropologically focused method is essential to the theological task.[4] The objectivist understanding of revelation is declared forthrightly:

> No uncertainty concerning the object of the church's scholarly task is possible. Every Christian community is under obligation through its dogma to one task: the knowledge of God is its goal, revelation is its object.[5]

It is ultimately the question of God which is the theologian's only concern and which unites all aspects of the theological task. Scholarly research and reflection which is not ultimately concerned with the question of God is quite simply not a part of the theological task. It is the question of God which makes historical study or anthropological reflection a part of the theological task. He writes:

> [The question of God] ...so commands our entire attention, and in as much as we discover an answer for it we receive the only specific knowledge that unites us as a religious community; which makes us church. On account of this all that the observational work of the dogmatician is occupied with stands under a complete, tightly integrated unity. Every object of the theologian's concern is dealt with from the perspective of how God is revealed through it.[6]

Clearly, Schlatter is intending something other than a theology of human self-consciousness when he declares that theology must be "anthropocentric". His disavowal of any such program is reflected in his many comments critical of Schleiermacher, and is expressly restated in the introduction to *Das Christliche Dogma*.[7] Theology *must* give its attention to religious experience and to the psychological dynamics of human existence, but it cannot *limit* its attention to experience without losing its subject matter and its distinctiveness as a discipline.

> The task of the dogmatician does not consist in the mere clarification of a part of the human spirit so that our self-consciousness is expanded and psychological or anthropological research is advanced. To have that as a goal would turn us away from the last and decisive question which religious experience presents to us. Theology's essential characteristic does not consist in the transmission of a series of marvelous feelings or ideas which create a particular formation of our consciousness or a noteworthy enhancement of our personal powers. Rather, religious

experience is truly present where the certainty of faith enters into us and becomes determinative of our attitude toward life. We do justice to religious processes only when we are led through them to the question of God.[8]

Schlatter, then, devotes a major portion of his dogmatic theology to the study of anthropology because he believes we will be ultimately be led through this study "to the question of God". And he believes we *must* be able to talk about anthropology as part of the theological task, precisely because the work of God (which is the real object of dogmatics) is *creative* of personal life. The work of God does not lead to a devaluation or a setting aside of our humanity. An anthropology must be developed as an essential part of the task of theology or we will find ourselves incapable of speaking intelligibly about the grace of God, and how through faith that grace becomes creative of personal life.

Schlatter's anthropology plays two critical roles within his larger theological work. First, it is critical for establishing his conviction that an awareness of God is a "given" in human experience and that this awareness sets the stage for perceiving and comprehending God's work in Christ; and second, it is a critical aspect of his epistemology because the rules or inner dynamics of personal life are the means by which he believes we make intelligible the inner dynamics of historical events. We will proceed by developing Schlatter's anthropology in relationship to the two critical roles that it plays within his larger thought.

The Origin of God-consciousness in Human Experience

When we enter into a discussion of Schlatter's understanding of how religious consciousness arises out of human experience, we encounter him at perhaps his most creative, or perhaps, idiosyncratic point. In Schlatter's own terminology his broad concern is to establish a multi-faceted "*Gottes-beweis*".[9] This concern for a "proof" of God is not for Schlatter simply a propadeutic to theology proper. His entire theological program is intended to ground and strengthen faith by demonstrating how it arises out of human experience. And we must recall again that his most common descriptive term for faith is *"Gewißheit Gottes"*. His whole concern in studying the New Testament and in reflecting on human experience in general is to show us how we come to a knowing, certain affirmation of God and through that certainty we come into a re-creative fellowship with God.

Schlatter has only minimal interest in the classic proofs for the existence of God because they do not fit his methodology. His method for a proof of God is the same method we have noted in his study of the New Testament. That is he sets out to *observe* how our awareness of God actually comes to be in human experience. Certainty about God is not derived from the conclusion of a syllogism, it comes to be because the reality of God the Creator is inextricably tied into every aspect of our life as personal beings. This is why Schlatter is just as hostile to fideism as he is to rationalism. A fideistic approach which makes our affirmation of God a wholly mysterious reality which can only be affirmed but never comprehended, violates the integrity of God's creation. Fideism makes faith out to be the negation of God's creative work, and Schlatter wants to see faith as the demonstration, par excellence, of the work of the creator God.

Schlatter's interest in human God-consciousness is no doubt partly inherited from the line of thought most closely associated with Schleiermacher. But in Schlatter's hands the discussion of God-consciousness takes a significant turn away from Schleiermacher. In Schlatter's opinion Schleiermacher limited God-consciousness to the area of feeling. This narrowing of focus had unfortunate consequences. First, it made awareness of God a pure, underived and thus unexplained a priori residing in the isolated individual. Schleiermacher does not establish the reality of God-consciousness by showing how it arises, he simply postulates it as a given in human awareness. Second, that means that the consideration of religion tends to become isolated from the question of truth, and unrelated to nature, history and community.[10] In a discussion of Schleiermacher, Schlatter writes, "The concept of God receives a different content depending on whether it simply designates the ground of our feeling of dependence or

if it refers to our actual dependence".[11] Schlatter's intent is to ground
human awareness of God in *all* aspects of life and to show that the very
existence of personal life presupposes a creator God. He will in turn ground
his "proof" in the inner make-up of the person; in our relationship to nature;
and in our relationship to history and community. While Schlatter develops
his proof in each of these areas in great detail, we must content ourselves
with a general summary that gives something of the character of his work.

For Schlatter we know God as creator because we know ourselves
as creatures.

> ...the certainty of our creatureliness determines our consciousness from the
> very beginning. The knowledge which we all have that we are not the
> source of our lives, but rather that another has made us, shows us that our
> self-consciousness and God-consciousness are inextricably linked
> together.[12]

Schlatter even has a rather ingenious way of arguing that this realization that
we are "made" cannot be reduced to the obvious point that we have parents.
He notes that the separate functions of the male and female in reproduction
is a sign that both are dependent on a higher power that enables them to
co-operate in a fruitful way![13] This realization that we are creatures, and
that we receive our life from a higher creative power shows that our
awareness of God is not rooted in our individuality. Our life is possible only
because there is a basic unity to life. Our inner life is a diverse but unified
whole, our life is only possible because it is integrated into the whole of
nature, and into the whole of human relationships and community. Yet none
of the human or natural elements within this whole is in itself capable of
creating all of life as a unity.

Schlatter gives expression to the fundamentally historical and
communal basis of our God-consciouness when he writes...

> We do not relate God's work only to the individual member of humanity,
> as if dependence on Him were a property of our particular individuality.
> Rather we relate it to the whole just as we do to ourselves. We note that
> the very foundation of our God-consciousness is universal.[14]

While Schlatter's focus goes beyond the individual, he spends a good deal of time showing how God-consciousness is the basis of all aspects of the inner life of a person. He works constantly with the concept of the person as a unity which integrates the three functions of thought, feeling and will. His concern is to demonstrate that each of these functions leads us inescapably to an awareness of God, and even more importantly, he seeks to demonstrate that only in relationship to God can these three aspects of the person function normally and as a harmonious unity.

Schlatter's discussions of the nature and unity of our inner life almost always begin with the role of thought and the question of truth.[15] The activity of human thought, in Schlatter's understanding, leads us ineluctably to an awareness of God. When confronted with an idea we find we are compelled to affirm or to reject it. This compulsion, or necessity to affirm or deny, to declare as true or untrue, Schlatter refers to as "the law of thought" (*Denkgesetz*).[16] We affirm something as true when we find we can integrate it into our previous experiences and understanding, and we reject it as false when we cannot. The question of the thing-in-itself lies beyond our vision. Our only obligation is to compare new ideas with the store of experiences and ideas that are already a part of our life, and to affirm or deny whether the new ideas can be integrated into a unity with what we already have and know to be true. If we try to both affirm and deny we encounter an "inner protest" which cannot be endured.[17]

This inner protest arises because all of our intellectual activity aims to create a unity. Our intellectual activity comes under the rule and authority of the concept of "unity".[18] Where the necessity of unity is denied or struggled against we lose our capacity to think and to judge. Schlatter also finds that we stand under an inner necessity to use the concept of causality. We can only affirm something as true where we have inquired into its causes, and compared and integrated it with other phenomena.[19] To only deal with reality as appearances and to cease to inquire into the ultimate origin of things is to surrender the question of truth.

Schlatter's understanding of thought as comparison of our already existing experiences and understandings with new experiences and ideas, leads him to the insight that thought also demonstrates to us our fundamental dependence. The affirmation of something as true does not simply depend on our activity, or our constructive or syllogistic skill. In order to know truth we are first of all obligated to observe. We know something to be true when we find ourselves compelled merely by observation of it to affirm it. We said earlier that for Schlatter knowledge consists of the two steps of "observation" and "judgment", and in both steps we find we are dependent on something that we have not created.[20] We are dependent on the reality of that which lies outside us because we must first of all observe it, and we are then dependent on the concepts of unity and causality through which we are enabled to make a positive or negative judgment. Only where both the tasks of observation and judgment are carried out in strict accordance to the laws of thought that are a part of our own inner life, can we be certain that our judgments are true.[21]

Schlatter believes we are driven by an inner necessity to observe and to make judgments, and that these judgments are only possible because our thought processes stand under certain imperatives that are not generated by nature or by human will. The activity of thinking leads us to God because:

> The law of thought does not arise out of nature. Indeed, nature does not think, but rather is an object for thought. Nor does it arise out of us because we constantly struggle against it and generate illusions.
> The law of thought is a given (*Es ist uns gesetzt*). The one who has imparted to us the calling to think and to know the truth, we call God.[22]

Or, as he explains it in *Das Christliche Dogma*, we know God as the creator of our ability to think and to make judgments, because in these activities, "we are guided by a law that is independent of us".[23] Since there is no way to explain the origin of the laws of thought from within the make-up of the person, the concept of causality itself compels us to see God as the ground of our ability to know the truth.

For Schlatter, "The fate of the idea of truth and the idea of God are identical".[24] If we see thought as dependent only on our activity we lose the deeper grounding of truth which gives us the confidence that our thinking can correspond to reality.

> When we have the certainty that we move about in a world which is thinkable, and that our thoughts have a positive relationship to the reality of the world, the concept of God is present.[25]

Schlatter's discussion of the role of feeling deals with it primarily as a mediator between thought and action. It is feeling that allows us to appropriate truth into our inner life and to convert intellectual affirmation into action. It is feeling that allows us to experience reality, not merely observe it.

Schlatter gives quite a bit of attention to the damage that results where thought and feeling are severed. He sees in the religious climate in the academic world of his time the belief that thought to be pure must be affect-less and unemotional, and that feeling severed from the question of truth is the root of religion. Science then deals with truth, and religion is a form of "*poesie*". Where religion is cut off from the question of truth it must inevitably lose an awareness of God. Religion then becomes an egoistical enhancement of the self. It serves only to meet the inner needs of the individual, but it is frustrated even in this because it has lost its relationship with the truth of a creator that transcends the self.[26]

Schlatter's treatment of feeling is varied and complex. He discusses a bewildering variety of feelings, and how they are related to other functions, and what ills befall a person whose feelings are disordered. At times it is difficult to know what purpose the discussion serves. It does not seem to lead as convincingly to a "proof" of God as does his discussion of thought. He discusses the feelings of fear and gratitude which we have in relation to God.[27] He has a good discussion of wonder, and suggests that all great intellectual endeavors are driven by the realization that we are confronted by that which is great and good, and that in this confrontation we realize that the good is not in us but stands "before us and over us".[28] He

also discusses joy and its power to overcome pain and despair, and its power
to motivate the will. The effect of his discussion of feeling seems to be to
show that in a variety of ways we encounter God through feelings, and that
the certainty of God is a powerful source of joy and wonder which bring
healing and wholeness to life. Without this sense of religious wonder and
joy the unity of our inner life is damaged, and the link between knowing the
truth and doing it is severed. While this hardly constitutes a proof of God,
Schlatter seems to be using it as a demonstration of our inner awareness of
God and to show that God-consciousness is intertwined with all of life
including the area of feeling.

Schlatter's discussion of the will is clearly the most conventional
treatment of any of the three aspects of personal life. In it he essentially
argues that we become aware of God through our awareness of an
unconditional moral norm that stands over against us.[29] While Schlatter
always begins his discussion of the person by describing the function of
thinking, it is clear that he sees will as that which lies at the center of
human identity. He discusses thought first because of his concern that
feeling and will never become divorced from the question of truth. Where
philosophy grasps "feeling" or "will" as the controlling function in human
life, and does not correlate those functions with thought, the individual
becomes isolated from history and community. Nevertheless, it is through
the function of will that we become creators; human life is actualized
through the act. Schlatter describes this relationship very clearly:

> While it is through knowledge and feeling that we receive the effects that
> the reality surrounding us presses upon us, it is through the activity of the
> will that we become the creator of effects with which we determine our
> own condition and effect the chain of events outside us. This is the highest
> expression of what has been given us. Here we touch the innermost
> essence of what it means to be human.[30]

And after noting the crucial role of the will, Schlatter asks rather rhetorical-
ly:

> Does an awareness of God arise at this point; at the point where our own
> creative powers become visible? Indeed, because our will contains a law;
> a law unto which it should unconditionally submit.[31]

Schlatter's discussion of the will, is once again, more subtle and detailed than we can trace at this point. And he sees the will as even more mysterious than thought or feeling. In particular, it remains a mystery how the will transmutes itself into action.[32] In the area of the will we become aware of God through our conscience. Though Schlatter acknowledges that the conscience is changeable and does not itself give us the moral norm, it remains as a formal structure that reminds us constantly of the reality of God.[33] Through our conscience we become aware of certain terms that express an unconditional, categorical obligation to do the good. Such words as "should", "duty", "bad", "good", and "guilt", express our awareness that the will out of which we generate action stands under an unconditional norm. What we become aware of as we contemplate these categorical terms is that we have not voluntarily generated them out of our own productive capacities.[34]

The conscience leads to a "proof" of God, which in a particularly powerful way demonstrates that God is a personal reality. It is because of our conscience that we clearly emerge as persons, in contrast to will-less nature. And since the categorical imperatives of the conscience are not generated by us, but are creative givens of our existence, they thus demonstrate that the ground of our being is a personal God. That which makes us uniquely human, at the same time shows us that we are dependent on a creator who is the source of the categorical norm. Our will is our very being—and at this critical point it is unmistakable that our being is dependent on another.

Because through our conscience we become aware of the fact that we are obligated to do what is right, we also at the same time become aware of our freedom.[35] We are not simply will-less material, nor are we an extension of divine reality. We stand over against God and through our conscience know that we are answerable to Him. Since we are thus accountable, our freedom and creative power as human beings is clearly established. Our conscience also shows us that we are not self-contained individuals, because through it we come immediately into contact with our neighbor. The conscience places us in immediate relationship to God, but is at the same time a social concept that brings us into immediate relationship with the larger human community.[36]

Schlatter also uses a negative argument for God-consciousness derived from the will; namely the reality of sin. Sin shows that we ourselves are not the source of a categorical norm, and yet our awareness of our sin and guilt shows that the norm is inescapable. In his treatment of this topic Schlatter sounds more like Luther than at any other point in his theology![37]

His "proof" for God, however, does not rest solely on the inner life of the person. He also develops a proof from nature. In *Das Christliche Dogma* that proof precedes his discussion of the person, and in *Die Gründe der christlichen Gewißheit*, the discussion of nature *follows* an extensive treatment of the person. We note his transition from the discussion of the person to the discussion of nature in *Die Gründe der christlichen Gewißheit*:

> ...so now we have become aware of the inner processes whereby the idea of God enters into our consciousness. ...But is it only our inner experiences that lead us down this road? Do we now enter into a conflict with nature, or does nature, too, direct us to the certainty of God?[38]

And once again the question is rhetorical. Nature presents us with a different challenge because it consists of unending lists of particulars and thus challenges the idea of unity that we find in the person. Nature also must be contrasted with the self because in nature we do not observe a will. Yet nature which lacks thought and will clearly evidences the fact that it is under the rule of laws, and thus clearly testifies that there is a supreme power which has *thought* nature. Nature is perhaps the simplest and most obvious source of our awareness of God.

> Nature is an unending display of intellectually penetrable and lawfully ordered power, and as such it is the first and most overwhelming witness to God. Therefore the affirmation of God as creator is a basic characteristic of our God-consciousness.[39]

We have now to some extent described Schlatter's understanding of the person as a unity of thought, feeling and will. We have ignored many of the nuances that he himself draws out of the discussion, particularly how the three functions are related and how the breakdown of the unity of the "life-act" destroys our capacity to be fully human. We have focused our discussion on how each of these functions leads us to and is grounded in God-consciousness. Throughout the discussion it is obvious that Schlatter has both apologetic and polemical motives. He wants to demonstrate that the religious question cannot be suppressed in any area of endeavor, and he wants to show how the historical methodologies of the day arise out of and contribute to a breakdown of the unity of the life-act, and thus to a loss of God-consciousness.

Schlatter is clear that none of his proofs for God constitute anything near to formal logical proofs for the existence of God. Such a proof is not his concern. His intent is to lead us through the processes in human experience which lead us to an awareness of God, and his goal is to lead us to a recognition of these dynamics in our own experience. All of these "proofs" can be denied, and all of them are resisted. And in and of themselves all of these "proofs" are fruitless. The realization of God that comes to us through many aspects of human experience does not in itself prove itself by decisively showing us God's creative power. Only through God's grace in Christ is personal life redeemed and recreated as a unity. But since for Schlatter God's grace in Christ is creative of personal life it does not negate, but rather clarifies and establishes that which we know of ourselves and God through human experience. The God who redeems us in Jesus Christ is our Creator, and His redemptive work establishes rather than negates His creative work.

Personal life and Historical Judgments

We had earlier alluded to the idea that Schlatter's anthropology plays a critical role in his historical methodology.[40] Having discussed his anthropology we may now be in a better position to explain what this means.

We must bear in mind that for Schlatter, while the historical task of theology is more "objective" than the dogmatic work of the theologian, the historian is also a person. The historian is a living subject engaged in the work of "observation". While the focus must always be on the historical subject-matter being observed, the observer can never, and should never seek to escape their own subjectivity. History itself is a personal reality which does not follow the law-like regularities of nature and which therefore cannot be understood by merely ordering events into an external cause-effect continuum. The essential "inner" continuities of historical events can only be grasped because the inner life of the historian provides analogies which make past personal life comprehensible.

Schlatter states this relationship clearly in, of all places, his discussion of the trinity.[41] The trinity, he points out, is not and cannot be derived merely from an analysis of our own inner life. The trinitarian name of God arises out of our observation of God's work in history. But the comprehension of what is given to us in history is possible because of the availability of analogies which arise out of our own personal life.

> They [God's acts] are comprehensible to us by virtue of the fact that between that which history shows us and our own inner life-act there exists an analogy. It is through this analogy that we are made able to interpret the historically given.[42]

This "analogy" from our own life-act which makes historical understanding possible consists of the inner dynamics of the person that have been outlined above. It refers to our make-up as persons constituted by thought, feeling and will, and our realization that the unity of the life-act has been broken by sin. It also refers to what Schlatter often calls "the laws of thought" which are givens of our personal being. Among these "laws" are the necessity of seeking for unity within ourselves and between ourselves and God and our neighbor; the necessity to understand things by reference to their ultimate cause; and our need to affirm something as either true or false. Schlatter is fully aware that the criteria for truth that he uses are not external objective measurements of the thing-in-itself, but rather they are measurements and activities drawn out of our subjectivity. He discusses this at length in his *Briefe über das Christliche Dogma*, especially in letter #4 entitled "Truth and Error".[43] In this letter Schlatter is responding to his imaginary correspondent's suggestion that while Schlatter is extremely critical of Kant, in the final analysis they share a great deal in common. The correspondent has pointed out that Schlatter derives his concepts of truth and error out of the inner consciousness of the person.

> [You point out]...that I develop the concepts of truth and error out of relationships that arise in our consciousness and use those as laws of thought. That is, I call something true if it corresponds to the laws of thought, and false if it is in conflict with these laws. You observe correctly that I find the measure of truth and error within our inner life; that is within our own inner organization which is given to us, and which sets the norm for our own productive work.[44]

This subject derived approach to understanding is unavoidable because the "thing" is not accessible to us, and because we as personal beings are not pure thought. The activities through which we come to historical understanding and make historical judgments are derived from our own consciousness, "because we never think without consciousness, but only through consciousness; we never see without the eye, but only through the eye."[45]

However, Schlatter's approach must be distinguished from that of Kant on a number of significant grounds. Kant's categories are merely forms or abstractions derived from pure reason which allow us to order quantifiable events in an externally connected series. Schlatter's "laws of thought" are derived from our personal being and encompass thought, feeling and the will. These categories enable us to reach across time and space to comprehend the inner, personal dynamics of history. Schlatter also differs from Kant in that he does not seek to understand history by organizing appearances in the correct causal sequence. For Schlatter history is mediated through language, and the object of historical observation is the words with which the historical witnesses recall and pass on the living effects of historical events. The biblical historian primarily observes and assesses the *claims* that are mediated to us through the language of the apostolic witness. And finally, Schlatter differs from Kant in that he does not apply his categories to only the phenomenal realm. The question of causality cannot be arbitrarily broken off at the limits of phenomenal reality without destroying our inner drive to understand and to know truth. The question of divine causality cannot be suppressed, because it too is a category that we find within our own personal being (see pp. 110ff. above). If the story of the Christ and the rise of faith in the early church can only be comprehended as a unity through affirming that God was the agent at work in Christ and in the sending of the Spirit, then we are compelled by the inner drive for truth and unity to make that affirmation. To stop the search for understanding and truth at any point should create a "protest" within our "intellectual conscience".[46]

I mentioned earlier (p. 107) that in a sense, faith, for Schlatter, is a historical judgment. It is a judgment or decision based on our "observation" of the story of the Christ, but also on the encounter that takes place between our life-act and the life-act of the Christ. That is, on an intellectual level (though not only on the intellectual level) faith is the judgment that God is at work in Christ for our redemption. That intellectual judgment is required by "the law of thought" that seeks for the ultimate cause of every historical reality. But the decision of faith also takes place on the level of feeling and the will. As we encounter the life-act of the Christ, we find the sinfulness of our own will and the brokenness of our life-act revealed, and as our sinfulness is revealed we also come to find that in Christ our life-act begins to be healed. Faith comes about as a convergence of what we observe in the story, and what we experience as a person whose life-act is judged and healed through the story of the Christ. Faith is described primarily by Schlatter as "certainty" (*Gewißheit Gottes*), and this certainty is planted by the Spirit within our inner life and there becomes a source of healing and re-integration of our "life-act". The knowledge of Christ, and the historical judgment regarding the truth or falsehood of the biblical claims about Christ, is inseparable from the interpreter's own encounter with the biblical story and its claim upon his entire inner life, including feeling and the will. A neo-Kantian critical approach to scriptures suppresses the question of truth by bracketing out the question of God, as well as by bracketing out the personal identity of the interpreter behind the screen of intellectual objectivity. The New Testament cannot be understood through pure reason, because it addresses itself to and claims our will. Finally, a neo-Kantian critical methodology destroys the person's capacity to understand and believe in the story of the Christ.

The Task of Dogmatics

Dogmatics has the task of deepening faith by clarifying how faith came to be.[47] The historical task of theology is to selflessly observe the biblical story, but the dogmatic task completes the historical by bringing into view the means whereby the Spirit planted faith in the believer, and what effect that faith will have in the believer's life. The task of dogmatics is to correlate the historically given with human experience. But this division of labor puts it too simply.

In Ch. III (endnote #26) we noted that the historical task points away from us toward the historical subject-matter. However, Schlatter adds the significant point that that does not mean that our subjectivity is not already operative in the historical task. The dogmatician is already present and active providing the historian with interpretive categories. But only in dogmatics itself do you investigate the interpretive categories.

> The connection between historical science and dogmatics, between the experience of others and that of oneself, between history which happened once and the history which is happening now, cannot be set aside until historical work is complete--as though only its completed results are instructive for the dogmatician, and determine his judgments. That would be to perceive only a half of what is going on here. The relationship between the two functions is there right from the beginning of historical work, and it is a matter of inter-reaction.[48]

What the dogmatician offers the historian from the very beginning of the historical task is the anthropological dynamics we have been describing in this chapter.

> The dogmatician in us supplies the historian with the capacity for making judgments through which he distinguishes between what is possible and what is not, and between what in the outline of history produces effects and what is dead.[49]

The explicit work of dogmatics begins, then, after the historical task is complete. Though to put it more accurately, in Schlatter's terms the historical task is not complete without dogmatics. The faith which arises through the observation of the story of Christ is creative of new life in a new community of love and service. And for faith to be creative it must be more than a life-less repetition of the biblical story. The creative and freeing power of God's grace in Christ itself demands our own productive and critical activity. God's grace creates life–and there can be no life if we are completely passive in our reception of that grace.

Since it is not the intent of this study to summarize the scope of Schlatter's dogmatic theology, perhaps it will suffice if we merely suggest the main aspects of the dogmatic task as Schlatter pursues it.

First, dogmatics critically retraces and analyzes the means the Spirit has used to bring the believer to faith. It shows how faith has arisen out of history and human experience. By tracing out this path dogmatics seeks to achieve a knowing understanding of faith which plants the certainty of faith all the more clearly within our own personal life-act. Even though the work of the Spirit is a mystery which transcends human observation, the Spirit works in and through the means of human experience and knowledge, and does not negate our own free activity in the process.

Second, dogmatics furthers the work of the Spirit by showing how grace takes form within our lives and brings about the healing of our life-act, both internally and in relation to God, nature and community. Dogmatics is a form of cultural criticism which enables us to understand the life destroying assumptions and attitudes that separate us from life-giving fellowship with God.

Third, dogmatics gives definition to basic Christian convictions by showing how they arise out of and give authentic expression to the story of the Christ. For Schlatter doctrines have no being in themselves apart from their function in expressing that which we know of God through what has happened in history and experience. It is the task of dogmatics to create new history by furthering the effects of the biblical story. To that end it seeks to express the central convictions which give form and life to the Christian community.

Excursus: Schlatter and Natural Theology

In light of Karl Barth's later attempt to draw the line between himself and Roman Catholicism and Liberalism at the point of their common affirmation of a natural theology, the question arises whether Schlatter would fall under the same judgment. Is this supposedly "biblical theologian" finally controlled by a philosophy of human experience that is derived from non-biblical sources?

Schlatter certainly took bitter exception to the extremes of early "dialectical theology". He mentions on one occasion that the apologetic devise of exalting God by denigrating nature is wholly misguided.[50]

But, Schlatter categorically rejects as a complete misunderstanding the charge that he, "grounds faith in Jesus on a natural theology and has renewed that old practice of 'theologia naturalis' as a propaedeutic to faith".[51] He begins his theology with the study of anthropology only because we as human creatures have no choice but to begin to think about everything by reflecting on our own life-story. But even here it must be remembered that his work in dogmatics was undertaken only after his two-volume *Theologie des Neuen Testaments*, was completed. Even though we have no choice but to think with and through our own subjectivity, the believer immediately confronts in their experience the story of the Christ, and that story so claims our attention that the first order of business is to observe the Christ story and to see how it originates in God.

> God's work lies hidden within the inner life, and it is only then perceived and understood when it becomes visible as God's work.[52]

Only after faith is understood as the work of God can the theologian return to reflect on human experience, and come to a deeper understanding of how faith comes to be, and how the genesis of faith is related to the human life-act.

As one reflects on the genesis of faith through the story of Christ, it becomes evident human subjectivity has not been negated or made passive in the process. While faith is mysterious, and in no sense the product of natural human capacities, it is also evident that natural human capacities for thought and judgment have been brought to play and have been the means of the work of the Spirit. The normal "laws of thought" that are given us from a creator God and which demonstrate our awareness of God, have been deepened and clarified through the act of observing and confessing the story of Christ. Faith does not negate, but rather sustains normal conditions of human thought and experience and action. So it is a part of the task of theology to help us understand what constitutes a genuinely healthy or rightly ordered humanity, and to give us insight into the various distortions and sicknesses which destroy the unity of the life-act.

The relationship of the study of anthropology and faith is explained by Schlatter in one of the more sensible quotes one will find on the question of theology and human experience:

> Being a human being is the presupposition for becoming a Christian... We are born as human beings and become Christian through our encounter with Jesus. But that is a completely different proposition than that which says that the study of anthropology is the condition for the establishment of the Christian understanding of life. When I say you are first a human being, then you become a Christian, I am not saying you must first comprehend your humanity and thereby because you have clarified that, you became a Christian. Such a proposition is completely foreign to my way of thinking.[53]

In letter #5 of *Briefe über das Christliche Dogma*, Schlatter deals with another question that logically arises from the foregoing discussion. His correspondent raises the question of Schlatter's "philosophical presuppositions", and asks whether his dogmatics are not derived from these pre-existing philosophical assumptions.[54] Schlatter responds by rejecting the idea of "presuppositions" as though his "philosophy" could be established somehow prior to the encounter with history. For him "the concrete always stands before the abstract." The question being addressed in this letter is whether the philosophical anthropology that Schlatter uses is a pre-supposition of his theology or a result of it. Is Schlatter's anthropology a time-less a priori through which he can interpret the biblical story? In that case would he not be denying his own insistence on the thoroughgoing historicity of even reason itself? Or is his anthropology derived from the biblical story? If so can he refer to these anthropological structures as means for assessing and determining the truth of the biblical story?

Schlatter rejects the idea that his anthropology is either a time-less presupposition, or merely a result of his theological convictions. There are no absolute beginnings in the process of human understanding. As he rather eloquently states it, "(I am) totally removed from the delusion that thought can ever tear the fabric of historical continuity and make an absolutely new beginning."[55] Schlatter gives full recognition to what later theologians might call "the hermeneutical circle". He cannot demonstrate the rational validity of his anthropology or prove that it is not derived from his own "life story" which includes a long history of being formed by Christian faith. Nor can he have an absolute historical method that allows him to understand the biblical history without drawing on the activities and resources that are a part of his own history. What is clear, however, is that faith is a new possibility that arises *within* human experience but not *from* human experience itself. Faith can only be understood as a work of God which takes place through the story of the Christ.

Endnotes

1.*Briefe über Das Christliche Dogma* (Stuttgart: Calwer Verlag, 2nd ed., 1978), 76.

2.*Das Christliche Dogma* (Stuttgart: Calwer Verlag, 3rd ed., 1977), 20.

3.Ibid., 14.

4.Ibid., 9–14.

5.Ibid., 11.

6.Ibid., 11.

7.Ibid., 558 and 569.

8.Ibid., 13.

9.Schlatter has extensive treatments of what he calls "Der Gottesbeweis" in three locations: *Die Gründe der christlichen Gewißheit* is a broad discussion of how we come to know God through all aspects of human experience. The anthropology section of *Das Christliche Dogma*, (pp. 20–279) is in its entirety an attempt to argue that human experience demonstrably attests to the reality of God. And in his *Briefe über das Christliche Dogma*, he discusses this question in letter #11 which is entitled, "Der Gottesbeweis".

10.*Die Gründe der christlichen Gewißheit*, pp. 55–56.

11.*Das Christliche Dogma*, footnote 17, p. 558.

12.Ibid., 26.

13.Ibid.

14.Ibid., 27.

15.In *Das Christliche Dogma*, after discussing the concept of personal life and the idea of a personal God (pp. 22–38), Schlatter then proceeds to a discussion of nature (pp. 38–61), human community (pp.61–89) and then discusses knowledge (pp.89–124), feeling (pp. 124–147), and then the will (pp. 149–198). He seems to take delight in detailed discussion of the interaction between thought, feeling and will and how Christ's work brings restored harmony between these three functions. In *Die Gründe der christlichen Gewißheit*, he discusses thought, feeling and will, respectively in chapters 4, 5 and 6 (pp. 40–65). In one of the more recently published monographs on Schlatter, *Der Gedanke der Einheit* (Stuttgart: Calwer Verlag, 1978) Irmgard Kindt presents the thesis that Schlatter's interest in the unity of the person is a continuation of the speculative philosophy of Franz von Baader.

16.*Das Christliche Dogma*, 90f.
  Briefe über das Christliche Dogma, letter #11, 30.

17.*Das Christliche Dogma*, 91.

18.*Die Gründe der christlichen Gewißheit*, 43.

19.Ibid., 44.

20.*Das Christliche Dogma*, 91.

21.*Gründe*, 45.

22.Ibid., 51.

23.*Das Christliche Dogma*, 100.

24.Ibid., 98.

25.Ibid.

26.*Gründe*, 55.

27.*Das Christliche Dogma*, 136.

28.Ibid., 129.

29.*Gründe*, 59.

30.Ibid.

31.Ibid.

32.*Das Christliche Dogma*, 157.

33.Ibid., 167–178.

34.Ibid., 169.

35.Ibid., 175.

36.Ibid., 178.

37.Following his discussion of the will, Schlatter often has a "proof" of God based on our awareness of sin. For example, pp. 66–73 in *Die Gründe der christlichen Gewißheit*, and pp. 220–222 in *Das Christliche Dogma*.

38.*Gründe*, 74.

39.Ibid., 77.

40.See my comments in Ch. VI, esp. pp. 120f.

41.*Das Christliche Dogma*, 354.

42.Ibid.

43.*Briefe über das Christliche Dogma*, 13ff. In these "letters" Schlatter responds to a variety of criticisms and questions that arose over his *Das Christliche Dogma*. He addresses all the letters in a personal way to a composite "critic" who has raised a variety of questions. The "critic" is not one individual, but is a devise that enables Schlatter to respond to all his critics without addressing anyone in particular. The tone of the letters is quite irenic with Schlatter often expressing appreciation for the "critic's" insight. They are a very ingenious and revealing collection of essays.

44.*Briefe*, 14.

45.Ibid.

46.Ibid., 15.

47.*Das Christliche Dogma*, 12.

48."The Theology of the New Testament and Dogmatics", from *The Nature of New Testament Theology*, ed. Robert Morgan., p. 126.

49.Ibid.

50.This idea is expressed quite strongly in Schlatter's hand-written comments in response to Bonhoeffer's *Bethel Bekenntnis*.

51.*Briefe*, #3.

52.*Rückblick auf meine Lebensarbeit*, 10.

53.*Briefe*, #14.

54.Ibid., 16.

55.*Briefe*, #5, 17.

Chapter VIII

CREATIVE GRACE

The thesis of this study is that the creativity of God's grace is the theme that provides the most adequate integration point for our understanding of Adolf Schlatter's theological method. We began in Ch. II with a discussion of theological method as an underlying concern in Schlatter's work and also formulated a preliminary statement of our thesis;[1] then in Ch. III explained how he developed a historical methodology for the study of the New Testament; and then in Ch. IV looked at how he applied that method to his study of the story of the Christ. In Chapters V-VII we attempted to penetrate more deeply into his methodology. Ch. V detailed his critique of rationalism and especially neo-Kantian "godless" methods. Ch. VI explored his philosophy of history and historical understanding, and then Ch. VII drew together his anthropology and how it functions in the theological task. In all of these we pointed ahead to a positive relationship between God as Creator and Redeemer; and thus toward a unity of revelation and human experience and a unity between faith and history. Or to state it negatively, we have seen how Schlatter opposes any theology or method that rends asunder what he believes God has joined together. We are now, perhaps, in a better position to fully state how the creativity of God's grace provides an integration point for all of Schlatter's work.

Schlatter's Luther Critique

We mentioned in "A Biographical Introduction" (p. 3 above), that Schlatter himself believed that the deepest motive of his work was "to complete the Reformation." He rather succinctly describes how this motive applied to his work as an exegete when he writes:

> How can the church gain free access to the New Testament? To achieve that I believe the criticism of the Reformation, especially of Luther, is absolutely essential.[2]

Schlatter sees himself as being in essential, though not uncritical continuity with the theology of the Reformation.[3] In particular he is in agreement with the Reformers in stressing the absolute prevenience of God in His relationship to the world. God is the Creator who accomplishes all things through the power of His Word. God is the gracious Redeemer who, motivated solely by His mercy, accomplishes our redemption for us in the work of Jesus Christ. And God's creative initiative continues as He brings us to a saving knowledge of Christ through the prevenient work of the Holy Spirit. Yet whenever Schlatter deals with the theme of prevenience he is more than likely to stress that the particular glory of God is not exhausted simply in His absolute prevenience. The nature and distinctive identity of the God who creates human life and redeems it by His grace is not adequately summarized, for Schlatter, unless one goes on to point out that it is God's particular glory not to be known merely as the prevenient One or as the One who works all things, but as the God who in His prevenience is *creative* of human life and history.

It is this emphasis on the creativity of God's grace that Schlatter perceived as the element of tension between himself and the Reformers, especially Luther. He saw in Luther an emphasis on the totality of human sin, and in stark contrast, the absolute prevenience of God's work in declaring the sinner justified, which had the effect of overemphasizing the passivity of the believer in faith and the Christian life.[4] He saw a tendency in Luther toward an egoistic perversion of faith where the justification of the individual is made the center of personal and theological concern, while Schlatter believed the New Testament went on to see the fulfillment of the Christian life in the Spirit's creation of a community of love and service.[5]

This incomplete view of grace, which failed to speak as clearly about the creativity of grace as about the prevenience of grace, produced an understanding of the church that identified it by its teachings rather than its works; that left the laity passive in the life of the church; and which did not manifest the new life that the New Testament claims is possible through Christ.

At the deepest theological level Schlatter regards this as a failure to realize fully the reconciling work of God in Christ, which not only judges the human will as sinful, but also shows to the sinful will another will, namely Jesus Christ's will to love and obedience which through the Spirit becomes a functional part of the believer. In Schlatter's understanding of the New Testament the believer actually enters into a working partnership with God.[6] Through the acceptance of God's judgment on sin and submission to Christ's will of love and obedience to the Father, the believer comes into an active covenant partnership with God in which first the will, but then with it thought, feeling and action are brought into a unity which allows the believer to realize the fully personal life of a creature made in God's image. Human life is, through grace, brought into a state analogous to divine creativity, and while it remains a creaturely and therefore derivative and dependent form of personal life, it is nonetheless a life actually reconciled to God in which the creature freely and knowingly becomes actively obedient.

If one were to state Schlatter's criticism of Luther in the strongest terms, one could say that he saw Luther still operating out of a sub-Christian understanding of God's redemptive work. Luther has not yet grasped the fullness of the reconciliation brought about through Christ and the Spirit, and still works from a framework in which the Spirit and the flesh, grace and the law, are estranged and alienated. But for Schlatter the redemptive life-act of the Christ is intended to create new life, and for grace to be creative it must be mediated to us through history and human experience, and must in turn take root in our life-act and become creative of a new history that takes form in a human community.

The Destructive Effects of Neo-Kantian Rationalism

Schlatter sees a continuity between the dualism in Luther's theology and the skeptical, secularized dualism found in Kant's critical philosophy and in neo-Kantian historical science.[7] Here the dualism takes the form of Lessing's opposition between the necessary truths of reason and the contingent truths of history, or it takes the Schleiermachian form of an opposition between that which can be known through critical rationality and that which the individual can intuit through feeling.

The overall effect of Kantian critical rationalism was to sever the interpreter's religious relationship to the biblical history. Since Kantian rationalism judged that reason could only understand phenomena and order them in an externally linked chain of causality that was limited to the time-space continuum, it studied history without reference to God as a causal agent and thus its eye grew blind to God's presence in history. Schlatter sets himself against the "history of religions" school that operated with this methodology and stated clearly what separated him from them:

> For them it was an essential conviction that the essence of religion was something other than historical. It was something individual which did not require a community in order to be. It was something timeless that was not affected by becoming. Religion was an idea or a feeling that belonged to the supra-historical essence of humanity. For that reason the presentation of the history of religion necessarily became a polemic against it. It ceased to be a revelation of God because anything that has sunken into the process of history, from their standpoint, can only become spoiled and confused.[8]

Schlatter saw it as his task to free the biblical scholarship of his era from this rationalistically based blindness to the presence of God in the contingent and time-bound. The critical rationalism that he opposed sought for scientific certainty in its study of history, and yet its ultimate religious effect was to make ultimate religious convictions not subject to public, disciplined canons of truth, but to leave these ultimate truth questions up to the subjectivity of the individual.

Schlatter's guiding conviction is that we exist as personal beings made in God's image, and as God's creation we are meant for existence in the time-bound contingent world of language, culture and community, and we are meant to live within the natural limits of human intellect and understanding. All these are the natural components of the life God has created for us to live. To make history barren of God's presence so that we can somehow meet Him in an immediate way through the intellect or subjective intuition sets us against the natural conditions God has set for our life. And it makes our religious knowledge unproductive. Timeless religious ideas, or immediate supra-historical intuitions of God cannot create a reconciled, unified life-act. Schlatter saw the heightened individualism of the modern era as a factor that severed our religious relationship to history, because it severed our understanding of how life is meant to be lived within the framework of community.

> We live our lives not as isolated essences, but only as members of the community out of which we arise and for which we live. God does not reveal Himself as the creator of individuals, but as the creator and Lord of His kingdom. God has made us through and for community.[9]

Schlatter contrasts his view to the description of the "history of religions school" stated above (p. 154) when he writes:

> God's work encompasses the entire condition of our lives. It gives us a new capacity to will and act and therefore has as its goal the creation of a community united by God. So even when I worked in systematics and taught dogmatics and ethics I was completely occupied with history. Though of course in these disciplines I was not occupied with past history, but with the history that we experience and create in the present.[10]

God's grace, Schlatter will insist repeatedly, does not negate the natural conditions of human life and understanding. As long as we are trapped by any form of epistemological dualism we cannot truly appropriate the personal and creative aspects of God's work. Schlatter writes, "The grounding of our life in the certainty of faith encompasses both the 'I' and its object; the knower and the known; the Spirit and nature."[11] Life cannot be lived simply on the basis of our historicity, but the Spirit creates life by working through the conditions of our historicity to bring us to an existential

certainty of God's grace, and through that certainty re-creates us within a
new community of faith and love.

Faith, History and Theological Method

Writing to his composite correspondent in his *Briefe über das
Christliche Dogma*, Schlatter turns a phrase that perhaps sums up his
understanding of his entire method. He writes, "You observe correctly that
the determining factor in all of my methodological decisions is given to me
with the certainty of faith."[12]

Grace is creative, and it creates human life anew by planting faith
in the inner consciousness of the person. In an utterance that is quintessen-
tially characteristic of both Schlatter's style and substance, he declares,
"*Glaube ist Gewißheit* (faith is certainty)."[13] It is this certainty of God's
grace toward us in Jesus Christ, that is the new creative event that brings
about a transformation of the believer's life-act, and enables him or her to
think, will and act in a way in a way that fulfills God's creative intentions.
Faith brings about a renewed unity to the life-act that had been severed by
sin and alienation.

Since faith is given birth through the creative grace of God, its
genesis can never be completely comprehended. The work of the creative
Spirit lies beyond our range of vision.[14] The certainty that faith has then
does not conform to the mathematical and rational models of proof that
dominated the science and philosophy of the Enlightenment. Schlatter's
concept of certainty is personal and creative, rather than mathematical and
solely cognitive. The theologian operates out of a personal "life-story" that
is the product of a community of faith, which is in turn a living effect that
proceeds from the "life-act" of the Christ. The believer approaches scripture
with a positive memory and expectation, and seeks primarily to penetrate
ever more deeply into the creative relationship between the biblical text and
the life of the believing community. The believer lives already from the

realization that the biblical text mediates the grace of God through the "life-act" of the Christ.

The sole imperative under which the Christian historian works is to observe biblical history so that the truth of the messianic claim of scripture can make itself visible. And the historian must guard him or herself from any unwarranted a priori concepts of historical method that forecloses the possibility of understanding the scriptures or the life of Jesus without reference to the work and presence of God.

The veracity of biblical truth claims is established then when they become a part of the believer's personal life in such a way that the person is recreated as a unity of thought, feeling and will within a community of love and service. The question of truth cannot be divorced from the experience of the believer. Schlatter goes so far as to say, "What the end result of a historian's work means for the historian depends on the history which takes place inside him."[15] The biblical message addresses the mind, but places its claim squarely upon the will. The question of truth is settled fundamentally by an act of obedience, in which the whole person gives trusting assent to the claim of the gospel. The peculiar characteristic of Schlatter the biblical historian is his insistence that even in the disciplined, scholarly study of scripture there cannot be a split between the intellect and the will without a loss of the ability to truly "observe" and thus hear the claim of the Christ. The "life story" of the historian ultimately limits and defines the way the biblical story is understood. There is, for Schlatter, no impartial methodology through which the community of scholarship can judge the truth claims of scripture. Judgment can only be exercised by fully personal lives who have heard the message of God's grace in Jesus Christ and have seen how that message addresses personal life. The historian's judgment of truth and the believer's decision for faith are one and the same process.[16]

So an essential move within Schlatter's method is to correlate the creative work of God in Christ with an anthropology which shows both the fundamentally historical and the inescapably theo-relational character of human existence. Schlatter presupposes a certain anthropology throughout his exegetical work, though it is only in his more reflective theological works that he gives direct attention to the topic.

For God's work to be creative it must be apprehended in and through the historical medium in which life takes place. Schlatter saw his mission as one of restoring to biblical scholarship the ability to see the presence and work of God within history. The historical character of biblical revelation and the inescapable historicity of human understanding is for Schlatter not a barrier to knowing God. Human existence within history itself raises the question of God, and the truth of the biblical revelation establishes itself by creating a new and reconciled history in which the individual person is healed and empowered to become a part of the community that is a continuation of the biblical story. A new community of faith and service is the effect for which the biblical story of God's grace in Christ is the only possible cause. In that it creates this living effect, the biblical story continues to establish its truth.

Faith is not imposed on the believer by a formal set of teachings carrying some kind of coercive power, nor is it grounded in my own autonomous will to believe. Faith emerges out of the convergence of my perception of the historical event of Christ's work, and the inner event of my self-consciousness of myself as a personal being. Faith as the convergence of the story of the Christ with our own personal life-act is demonstrated well by the following quote:

> In as much as the witness of God which comes to us from the outside binds itself with our own inner processes, we receive that which creates certainty.[17]

By this Schlatter does not mean the self considered in isolation. He rejects Augustine's formula "the soul and God", because when the soul is considered in isolation from nature, history, and community, "personal life dies".[18]

Schlatter catalogues the creative effects of grace in the following extended description:

> That which Jesus gives us has the effect that the unity which is implanted as a law in our personal life-act is established, and all disharmony with which we destroy our personal life-act is overcome. It also enables us to rejoice in the Creator who is evident in nature and allows us to place our trust in Him. It also allows us to become obedient to the divine governance which works through history to form and move us, thus enabling us to be united with history. And the fact that the history that we experience and create is creative (*heilsam*) of us and others, has the effect that the certainty of God illuminates and orders the entire content of our consciousness without thereby destroying our own thinking. And this has the effect that the divine law which continually guides and judges our own will comes to supremacy in us and separation from our perverted wills does not remain a mere wish, but rather we are led to faithful service to God. It has the effect that we attain a kind of community which strengthens and enables our life in its entirety, and thus makes fruitful our capacity to serve others.[19]

Schlatter's program in both his work as biblical interpreter and as dogmatician, is to demonstrate how the creative grace of God can heal the epistemological dead-ends that arise from both classic and modern forms of rationalism which ignore the contingent and time-bound and locate truth in the unchanging eternal realm or in the abstract operations of the mind. These epistemologies destroy faith because they destroy our capacity to observe history, and history is the means through which God works to mediate His creative grace to us. The history through which God works is what grounds and establishes faith, and it is faith that mediates God's work to us thus in turn creating a history in which we work in relationship to God. Historical study and understanding has a direct relationship to faith because, "it (history) has the power to create faith and produce certainty".[20]

The certainty of faith arises out of history, but is not merely the end product of the accumulation of historical data. Certainty is an inner and religious reality. In the following quote Schlatter raises and answers the question of the relationship of faith to historical knowledge:

> Faith is certainty. Can, however, certainty arise out of something from the past? The past is to a large extent lost in forgetfulness, and our efforts to create a clear historical picture necessarily remain highly incomplete and usually we arrive at nothing more than various levels of probability.

> It is only possible, but then it is indeed possible, to achieve a
> believing connection to the past, when it awakens the consciousness of
> God within us. That alone gives us the certainty that is free of all
> limitations. And to that end we do not require the knowledge of all events
> in their entirety... [21]

The inner meaning of the story of the Christ is opened to us, in the
final analysis, through the work of the Spirit, who recreates personal life
through the redemptive work of Christ:

> It (the Spirit) brings us to awareness of the creative grace (*schöpferische
> Gnade*) that grasps our inner person and places the certainty of God
> (*Gewißheit Gottes*) in our thinking, thereby bestowing on us the love that
> transforms our life into the service of God.[22]

The creativity of God's grace is ultimately the hinge that allows
Schlatter to see a unity between the biblical story and human experience. We
are created to know our Creator, and through the encounter with God in
Christ our capacity to see and understand is truly made fruitful, and in this
seeing and understanding of God in Christ our lives find their purpose and
fulfillment.

Concluding Observations

I believe that the reader who has followed the argument to this point
is convinced that Schlatter has established a highly original and broadly
comprehensive approach to the question of faith and history. There is both
a critical and a constructive side to his work.

On the critical side we have his criticisms of rationalism in the
history of theology, and in particular his decisive criticism of a historical
critical methodology based on neo-Kantian epistemological assumptions.
Here his work shows a depth of insight that is really far ahead of his time.
In fact, so deeply ingrained were the dogmas of neo-Kantian rationalism that
the price Schlatter paid for rejecting them was being ignored by many as a
serious academic theologian. Schlatter does not look as naive at the end of
the twentieth century as he did at the beginning of it.

But Schlatter put most of his energies into a constructive effort to heal and rebuild the biblical scholarship of his day. Here his efforts are very suggestive of further possibilities, though many of the specifics of his methods and conclusions would not endure. Schlatter worked to establish an essential unity to the message of the New Testament, and saw a complete continuity between the story of the Christ, and the theology of the apostolic community. This unity and continuity of thought is not entirely pre-critical. Schlatter was aware, for example, that the apostolic community had a decisive role in shaping the biblical story of Christ. But he did not subject his thesis of the unity of the New Testament to all of the critical tests that it would need to meet. One cannot help but have the impression that he moved over certain critical questions all too lightly.

Certainly a strength of Schlatter's constructive proposal is that it gives us a glimpse of how comprehensive a truly satisfactory theological method for our day would need to be. Schlatter seeks to genuinely correlate revelation and human experience, but in such a way that revelation is not taken captive by an a priori anthropological construct. He sought to accomplish both the tasks that Karl Barth and Paul Tillich set out to do in the next generation of theologians. His is neither a kerygmatic theology with only a tenuous link to human experience, nor is it simply an anthropology in which God appears as the depth dimension of human existence. This attempt to be both kerygmatic and experiential perhaps shows some similarity to current attempts at narrative theology. The "word of God" in Schlatter is not over and above the biblical text, rather the narrative structure of the text identifies Christ as he lived in and from God. And the narrative structure of the biblical revelation in some way correlates with the narrative structure of human experience. In fact the truth of the biblical story of the Christ is only confirmed as it transforms our story and creates a new history of faith and obedience. The Christian community is life lived as a continuation and expression of the story of God's grace revealed to us in Christ.

However, while Schlatter creatively addresses the question of a Christian anthropology, his approach at some times seems a bit obtrusive. One cannot help but feel at times that his concept of life as a unity of thought, feeling and will works almost *too* nicely toward meeting his own epistemological ends. A critical piece in his program is the idea that we can come to know God in the story of the Christ because our own inner life provides analogies which make understanding possible.[23] This may be a weak link in the whole structure. He may be making his anthropology carry more weight than it can bear. And while he often asserts that a fulfilled life is life in a community of love and service, he deals much more readily with the dynamics of the life of the individual than he does with the life of the individual within community. It is clear how Schlatter sees grace healing the individual and creating a unity between thought, feeling and will. But it is less clear how grace actually creates a new community of love and service in which the larger eschatological creative purposes of God are to some extent actualized.

But even with these questions and reservations, the person who comes to know and appreciate Schlatter's approach to theology finds themselves challenged once again to rethink how we approach the study of scripture, and how we conceive of God at work in the midst of human history.

Endnotes

1.See p. 26–27 above.

2.*Die Religionswissenschaft im Selbstdarstellungen*, p. 165.

3.Ibid. Schlatter states that he is in complete agreement with Luther's doctrine of justification and that in his time and place it was precisely the word that needed to be heard. He states that he "would not be presumptuous enough to stand in judgment on Luther". He does however want to ask whether it is still life-giving and timely to simply repeat Luther's word in the current situation.

4.Irmgard Kindt has done a major study of Schlatter entitled *Der Gedanke der Einheit* (Stuttgart: Calwer Verlag, 1978), which sharply criticizes his work from a Lutheran perspective. Kindt takes Schlatter to task for his rejection of Luther's concepts of sin and justification. Her thesis is that contrary to the common opinion that Schlatter was a creative and highly original biblical theologian, his work is actually a speculative philosophy derived largely from the thought of Franz von Baader and dominated by the concept of "unity". Despite the immense erudition and original research behind this book it is dominated by polemical interests and succeeds primarily in demonstrating that Schlatter was not a very good Lutheran—a point he would have readily conceded.

5.While Schlatter is reserved in his personal judgments about Luther, he can be biting in his criticism of the kind of piety that he sees arising from Luther's influence. My favorite comment is where he mockingly describes a piety which sees our life, "as a journey of tears until we reach a blessed death." Another good one is found in his essay "Natur, Sünde und Gnade", (p. 50) where he says that a faith which flees from nature and history, "leads us to a piety of meditation in the church of the gnostics, theologians and preachers; while the other leads us to a piety of deeds in the church of the servants, the church of the apostles."

6.*Die Religionswissenschaft der Gegenwart im Selbstdarstellungen*, 155. Here Schlatter refers to the church as a "community of work" (*Arbeitsgemeinschaft*), within which we fulfill our lives in a many-faceted giving and taking.

7."Atheistische Methoden", 238. In his discussion of Jäger's proposal for a historical study of the scriptures using "atheistic methods", Schlatter writes, "If one looks into the overall inner make-up of Protestantism it is not entirely surprising that Jäger can so easily complete this rending asunder (of faith and history)."

8.*Selbstdarstellungen*, 162.

9.*Das Christliche Dogma*, 20.

10.Ibid.

11.*Selbstdarstellungen*, p. 154.

12.*Briefe über das Christliche Dogma*, #8.

13.*Die Gründe der christlichen Gewißheit*, 92.

14.For an extended discussion of this topic see ch. VI, p. 114–116.

15."The Theology of the New Testament and Dogmatics", 129.

16.Schlatter believes that in this area, as in many others, we learn by doing. In his "The Theology of the New Testament and Dogmatics", (p.127) he writes, "I believe we are given a capacity for seeing. But this cannot be proved to someone who denies it. The rule 'Do and you will know' applies here. As is the case with all fundamental convictions, *action* is the potency which shapes our consciousness."

17."Der Glaube und die Geschichte", from *Gesunde Lehre*, Freizeiten Verlag zu Delbert im Rheinland, 1929, 348.

18.Ibid., 349.

19.*Briefe über das Christliche Dogma*, #8, p. 39.

20."Der Glaube and die Geschichte", 341.

21.*Die Gründe der christlichen Gewißheit*, 92–93.

22.Ibid., 109.

23.See our discussion in Ch. VII, p. 142f.

APPENDIX A

A translation of pp. 364–372 from the chapter "Die Schrift", from
Das Christliche Dogma.

(*Note: The footnotes are from Schlatter.)

The Scriptures

In every period of time the apostles ground and guide the church through the scriptures. This takes place through the New Testament which they authored, as well as through the Old Testament which they along with the church passed on as their scriptures. Since the church possesses the apostolic scriptures it remains always under their guidance and has no need for an apostolic office. This view of the scriptures follows from the task which was assigned to the prophets and apostles.

a. The Origin of the Scriptures from the Spirit

Just as every personal relationship to God is mediated through the Holy Spirit, so the apostolic and prophetic task has its basis in the fact that the Spirit of God imparted to those who are called their capacity to think, will and act. Only in this way can there be a history that has its basis in God; or a word through which God calls us.

The inspiration of the scriptures is misunderstood when it refers only to their intellectual correctness. The doctrine of scripture took on this twist first in the synagogue, and from there was transmitted to the church. This misunderstanding took place because they saw the scriptures as being above all a medium of knowledge through which we acquire the ideas related to our relationship with God. From this approach to scripture it follows that the doctrine of inspiration refers to God's having supplied the authors with their knowledge. This view of the scriptures rests on the correct observation that the church approached the work of Jesus with utmost concern for truth, and it honored the truth as God's gift. The church was concerned for a knowing and thoughtful turning toward God, and guided thought toward understanding and certainty. Because the scriptures are a means of grace they are also a means of knowledge. However, a dangerous confusion threatens us if they are used only as a medium of knowledge. They do not give knowledge only for the sake of our intellectual enlightenment, nor only as a gift to our intellect, rather they offer us God's grace in its fulness, and are intended to promote faith and create love. They address not only our intellect but our entire life situation. The scriptures are a teaching book *because* they are the call and offer of God's grace to us. They are a resource for theologians and scholars because they show us God's work to recreate us as children of God, not only as thinkers.

The doctrine of inspiration does not refer to the truth of this or that concept, rather it refers to the fact that the scriptures form and change persons so that they are enabled to speak the word of God. As long as the doctrine of inspiration referred only to scripture as an intellectual medium, it still implied alienation between God and humanity and worked out of the pre-christian way of thinking which thought of God and humanity as enemies. Therefore the Spirit, since He is holy and is God, must work as a negator of that which is merely human. The activity of the Spirit requires the passivity of the one who is inspired; his own consciousness is submerged and his own will is silenced, he is moved as the harp is by the player or as the pen is moved by the writer. So understood the act of inspiration is an isolated experience that simply inserts itself into normal human processes and shares nothing in common with them. The unity of the life-act is broken by the event of inspiration.

This is an understanding of the Spirit which is not yet measured by Christ, or by what we ourselves can see in him, or by what God's grace has accomplished for us. In Jesus we come face to face with the way that God intends for divine inspiration to be related to human reception. In him we see the fulness of the Spirit, and the Spirit creates in him humanity in all its fulness. This arises because God wills through the Spirit to bring our humanity to creative activity which serves Him. So the humanity of the God-man is not drained to a state of lack of awareness and passivity, but rather is called and empowered to act. By this means the grace of God is carried into the world. In the same way, the promise of Jesus is imparted to the believer so that through the Spirit the believer is not negated, but is born anew. The believer receives life through the Spirit and not in such a way that they become a will-less slave who has not internalized the power and task they have received.

As long as the unreconciled condition of humanity is assumed, the idea that God touches persons in such a way that they become active agents, appears to be unbelief. From this view, divine revelation is conceivable only if the person in communion with God is reduced to an inanimate tool. That is why this concept of inspiration limits the work of the Spirit to the intellect and reduces God's inspiring activity to the dispensing of ideas. If the capacity for thought is the sole arena in which God witnesses to Himself, then it is even desirable that the person himself be anesthetized so that only his capacity for thought can function, and then only under the direct guidance of the Spirit. However, God's grace affects not only our ideas, but us as persons. His call is not only to our intellect, but confers on us a fellowship of will and work with Him. Therefore, the Spirit of God works in us, not in a way that destroys our humanity, but in a way that brings us to life.

The ancient doctrine of inspiration is motivated by a valid theological intent in that it leads the reader of scripture to direct his gaze solely on God. In the scriptures we are not to think of the human witnesses and their peculiarities, rather we are to hear God through them. In this sense the ancient doctrine of inspiration is an expression of faith.[211] But in this

---

[211]The traditional doctrine of inspiration was motivated by faith, so it not only continued, but was even strengthened through the course of the Reformation. It was strenthened because the word of judgment directed against the church only had validity if it possessed a basis and proof in a holy, revered canon. Therefore the authority of scripture was never more urgently important as in the church struggle that was initiated by the Reformation. This way of thinking was strengthened because the Reformation sought to ground faith solely in Christ and not in the church. For that reason it sought to build only on the scriptures.

doctrine of scripture everything that brings to mind the humanity of the messengers appears only in a problematic light, as though we must always look beyond their humanity to God in order that we may find that which we are looking for.

This belief is in a sense confused. It seeks a union with God, and yet it does that by distancing us from God's revelation and reign. But in actuality faith is only a possibility if everything else is not eclipsed by God's light. Faith is possible only if we as persons are not rendered speechless by God's speech. Instead, our speaking becomes a possibility and in God's service we learn to speak and think. The result of God's revelation is not that God is enclosed in His solitude so that He has no space for anyone but Himself, but that he enables humanity to become truly active and alive. If God's revelation were delivered in any other manner then we could not have faith in Him; we could not lay hold of God's grace as that which gives us life.

Of course, our interaction with the scriptures is fruitless when we hear only the fascinating human characters in it, or when we read it as the history of ancient religions, or the products of religious genius. The prophets and apostles speak as God's witnesses and are only heard by us when we recognize their calling. Our thought and will in conversation with the scriptures does need to be directed toward God, but not in a way that detours around the human witnesses, but precisely in and through their service.

Out of a doctrine of inspiration which separates inspiration from human activity, arises the separation of scripture from history. History then appears as a hindrance to the Spirit's work and therefore is not merely ignored but is struggled against. There then emerges an antithesis to the ancient doctrine of inspiration, which recognizes that we can observe even in biblical characters and writings the normal historical relationships and dependencies which form all of history.

This leads to a polemic against the ancient doctrine of scripture, and to an approach that seeks to explain the Bible only through its historical characteristics, or sees the Bible only as a set of historical documents that make the early life of the church accessible to us.[212] The acceptance of an opposition between history and the work of the Spirit is just as false when history is set against the Spirit as when the Spirit is set over against history.

We must move beyond this opposition and recognize that in an adequate approach to pneumatology and to history both belong inseparably together. It is through the history, of which the biblical characters are a part, that we receive the Spirit. The inspiration of the apostles is grounded in Christ and arises out of his history. The Spirit leads us into history, not out of it, because He does not bring about the impoverishment of human life, but rather brings forth authentic humans whose thought and will proceed from God because they think what God thinks, and will what He wills. Therefore God *creates* history; history as the mutually conditioned life and relationships that are joined together to form a community; history as the joining of life into a chain of tradition which continues to form subsequent life. This does not entail a belittling of the work and power of the Spirit, but is precisely that which the Spirit wills and works. For that reason, the effective power of the scriptures consists in how they emerge out of history and how they continue to create history. Scripture creates history in that it brings to our thought and will the reality of what happened in the past so that our present life receives its form and content from it.

That means that reference to the Bible only as a historical source or record of the past is not adequate. It does not offer us the past only so that

---

[212]There are several precedents for this, including Häring (Der Christliche Glaube, 172f.), although he emphatically stated that for evangelical Christianity the contemporary relationship to the scriptures continues to be a vital issue. This is certainly to the point because the formula that is used to describe the origin of scripture also gives us the norm for their use. Behind the pre-christian idea of inspiration stands a ruling teaching office, whether it be the rabbinic school, a priesthood or a theological faculty that tends to the correct interpretation of scripture. Behind the inspiration concept of the apostles stands the community that expresses its conviction that the same Spirit that speaks in the scriptures is also at work in them. Behind the formulation that regards the scriptures as a collection of historical documents stands the unbelieving, Spirit-denying historian who reduces everything that the scriptures describes to that which always and everywhere occurs. This demonstrates the widely held judgment that ones judgment concerning the scriptures contains within it the self-understanding of the church.

we can study and remember it, rather it seeks to present history in a way that conditions and claims our history so as to bring us into community with God. Out of past experiences come our own experiences. And in that the scriptures lead us to a our own experience of the grace of God they prove themselves to be the work of the Spirit.

As long as the doctrine of inspiration and the historical understanding of scripture are in opposition, the realities that the scriptures offer to us cannot be truly perceived. Either we conjecture up a so-called history in which humanity creates its own religion and discovers its own God, or a so-called Spirit, but one who holds Himself aloof and separate from the concrete content of human experience. The Spiritless and therefore Godless interpretation of scripture is not science, nor is an ahistorical and therefore inhuman interpretation.

In order to bring human life and creativity into the relationship of God with His messengers, the relationship of inspiration to the *words* of the the messenger (signified by the term "verbal inspiration") must be rejected, and the *person* must be described as the object of inspiration. The idea that the words are simply dropped into the personal life-act of the messenger is to be set aside. However, with this rejection of a central emphasis on the words, an even darker possibility emerges. And that is the idea that what the scripture really has to offer us behind its words is a yet to be discovered "kernel", and that it is this word that we must seek out and uncover and which will determine whether or not we are made one with God.[213] If the Spirit is held distant from the words of the apostles then the Spirit is also separated from God's work, because His work is accomplished through the word. That would mean that God is alienated from our work and relation-

---

[213]When Paul calls his word God's power unto salvation for everyone who believes, and when he counts the word of reconciliation that has been entrusted to us as God's work of reconciliation (Romans 1:16, II Cor. 5:19), he is not thinking of some content hidden in his words, but rather of the exact words that he says. It is exactly the same when God gives life to us through the word of truth (James 1:18), or when Jesus makes participation in the kingdom of God dependent on his words (Mt. 7:24, 13:3f.). There is no content apart from the word that serves as the means of grace, rather the word that comes to expression carries the grace of God into the hearer's situation.

ships because these take place through the word. But because the Spirit calls and enables the messengers of God, His gift to them must be in speech.

b. The Unity of the scriptures

The unity of the scriptures is important because it is the means whereby they are recognized by us as the word of God. Unity is the mark of God. It is He who has planted in our thought the rule which compels us to reject contradiction. And He has planted in our will the rule that something is not good when it divides us and creates discord, and the rule that Christ is given to the community in order to create a humanity reconciled to and in God. If the scriptures are to help us to this goal, their word must not be destroyed by contradictions that lead us into discord.

That does not mean that it is the task of scripture to serve a primarily rationalistic goal. Scripture is not a means by which we construct a unitary, complete system of ideas, as though that were the goal of our lives. The Bible does not empty our lives by reducing them to the dialectical play of abstractions. It knowingly leaves gaps in our understanding and does not regard that as a lack or impoverishment. However, the need for unity as a good and a goal in our life does not simply arise out a rationalistic ideal; it arises out of the inner make-up of us as persons. So the scriptures could not be life-giving to us, but would be burden for our lives, if it carried contradictions into our life.

But here, as overall, the demand for unity often reduces itself to an empty Oneness that drives diversity and richness from itself. The reformer's use of scripture never overcame the tendency to see everything in the Bible as being on the same level, and that each word of scripture needs to be read and interpreted as every other word. Since it all carries the absolute authority of God, it appears that all variety is ruled out. But in as much as the interpretation of scripture is captivated by this view of scripture, the tendency to harmonize the words actually weakens and hinders its power.

The unity of scripture consists in the fact that both the history that is in scripture and the history that it creates has its unity in Christ. The recognition of Jesus as the Christ also gives expression of the subordination of the apostles and prophets to him. The center of scripture which makes it a unity is well expressed in Luther's formula; "was Christum treibe, sei kanonisch".[214] This expresses not only that there is a border between scripture and other voices, but it also means that within the scriptures the individual parts have their place and order of significance and effectiveness. However, this idea is misused when it is used to assert that only the explicit proclamation of Christ is valid as the word of God, or that the Old Testament is only valid where it contains direct messianic promises. So understood, the messianic work of Christ is strengthened by negating everything that is less than that, so that the prophets and apostles are nothing where they are not describing him. In this way the concrete unity of the scriptures is again replaced by an empty oneness of message.

In the formation of the judgment as to what extent a part of scripture is a witness to Christ attention must be given to how its contents stand in relationship to the work of Christ. For example, the law serves him because we cannot understand his mission unless God's will as something in opposition to our will has been made known to us. The book of James with its concept of repentance leads to Christ who rejects all religious pride and humbles us before God. But we can clearly observe gradations between different persons and times, and these condition their meaning and message to us. They do not all guide us with the same clarity and completeness to our goal in Christ, and their significance must be measured accordingly.

Since the parts of scripture are of more or less significance we must ask the question whether we can determine different degrees of inspiration. Their differences, however, are not to be found in the relationship between the creative causality of God to the receiver of His message. Rather the distinctions need to be made through an evaluation of what their particular service is. What are the limits of their particular function? Not all of God's messengers have the same duty, therefore they are also given varying capabilities. But here the rule formulated by Paul is still valid; a member of

---

[214]In the "Vorrede" of Jakobus, e.g. 63,157.

the body that has a lesser function is still indeed a member of the body. Inspiraton is a creative gift of God, and is thus an absolute act which does not allow itself to be measured by degrees. No matter whether little or much is given, God is the giver. Synergistic interpretations are not of any use here because the activity of God is not dependant on human activity, but rather stands over and before it and is the source out of which it arises.

Ps. 19 gives expression to a simple idea. Should we, however, regard the work of the Spirit that gave rise to it as weaker than that which created the full understanding of Christian faith that we find, for example, in Romans 8? Is more Spirit required to pray to God in the form of Jesus than to God in the majesty of the course of the sun? Both entail a freeing of our view from its bondage to the world. In the one our view is freed from Baal, in the other it is freed from the offense that Jesus' rejection and cross created throughout Israel. In both the knowledge of God is His own work, a gift through which the creative power of God's grace enters into humanity. But the service that each of these texts provide us are not the same, because the one that shows us the Christ as the giver of righteousness and the Spirit gives us more than the text that describes the sun as God's messenger. The "Preacher" of Ecclesiastes, who suffered so much that all human values are reduced to nothing and he is left only with the fear of God, does not serve the same purpose as the epistle of John who describes the fulness of joy and love for us. But does that mean there is a lesser manifestation of God in one over the other? Even in Ecclesiastes, to see the nothingness of human existence and yet to not deny God requires the presence in the human spirit of an all-powerful divine grace.

The unity of the scriptures in their ground corresponds to the unity in their effect. From every point of scripture that we turn toward, we are lead toward a totality. They awaken in us not only one human function, but others as well, which taken together leads us to the fulness of the gift God has given. Within a particular period of time this principle may be upheld only with great difficulty and struggle. But the church has clearly experienced and learned that a sincere encounter with the scriptures cannot be limited to just one part. When the authority of scripture is recognized and committment to it is consistently carried through, it leads us into the fulness of God's grace.[215]

---

[215]"Whether you wish to speak of God's glory or knowledge of self or of sin and redemption through Christ or of the community of saints or about the unfolding of the last things, you finally will be lead by the spirit of Jesus into all truth. Who the son makes free is freed from all religious strife." Ötinger, *Biblisches Wörterbuch*, published by von Hamberger, p. 394.

SELECTED BIBLIOGRAPHY

Primary Sources

Major theological works:

Briefe über das Christliche Dogma. 2d ed. Stuttgart: Calwer Verlag, 1978.

Das Christliche Dogma. 3d ed. Stuttgart: Calwer Verlag, 1977.

Die Christliche Ethik. 5th ed. Stuttgart: Calwer Verlag, 1986.

Der Dienst des Christen. ed. Werner Neuer, Giessen/Basel: Brunnen Verlag, 1991

Die Geschichte des Christus. 3d ed. Stuttgart: Calwer Verlag, 1977.

Der Glaube im Neuen Testament. 6th ed. Stuttgart: Calwer Verlag, 1982.

Die Gründe der christlichen Gewißheit. Stuttgart: Calwer Verlag, 1927.

Metaphysik. Classroom lectures edited and with introduction by Werner Neuer. Published in *Zeitschrift für Theologie und Kirche,* Beiheft 7, 1987.

Die Philosophische Arbeit seit Cartesius. 4th ed. Stuttgart: Calwer Verlag, 1959.

Die Theologie der Apostel. 2d ed. Stuttgart: Calwer Verlag, 1977.

Autobiographical works:

Erlebtes. 5th ed. Furche Verlag, 1929.

Rückblick auf meine Lebensarbeit. 2d ed. Stuttgart: Calwer Verlag, 1977.

"Die Entstehung der Beiträge zur Forderung christlicher Theologie und ihr Zusammenhang mit meiner theologischen Arbeit zum Beginn ihres 25. Bandes dargestellt." *Beiträge zur Förderung christlicher Theologie*, 25. vol. 1 (1920).

Major Commentaries:

Der Evangelist Matthäus. Seine Sprache, sein Ziel, seine Selbstständigkeit. Stuttgart: Calwer Verlag, 1929.

Der Evangelist Johannes. Wie er spricht, denkt und glaubt. Stuttgart: Calwer Verlag,

Das Evangelium des Lukas. Aus seinen Quellen erklärt. Stuttgart: Calwer Verlag, 1931.

Der Brief Jakobus, ausgelegt. Stuttgart: Calwer Verlag, 1932.

Paulus, der Bote Jesus. Eine Deutung seiner Briefe an die Korinther. Stuttgart: Calwer Verlag, 1934.

Markus, der Evangelist für die Griechen. Stuttgart: Calwer Verlag, 1935.

Gottes Gerechtigkeit. Ein Kommentar zum Römerbrief. Stuttgart: Calwer Verlag, 1935.

Die Kirche der Griechen im Urteil des Paulus. Eine Auslegung seiner Brief an Timotheus und Titus. Stuttgart: Calwer Verlag, 1936.

Collected essays:

Gesunde Lehre: Reden und Aufsätze. Freizeiten-Verlag, 1929.

Hülfe im Bibelnot: Neues und Altes zur Schriftfrage. Freizeiten-Verlag, 1928

Articles: (listed chronologically as written)

"Kritik und Glaube." *Kirchenfreund* 15. #12 (Oct. 1881) 183ff.

"Aus dem inneren Leben der Schule Ritschls." *Kirchenfreund* 20. #26 Dec 1886) 409–417.

"Die Kirche und die negative Kritik." *Ev. Kirchenzeitung* 125. (June 1890) 449–454, 465–472.

"Die heilige Geschichte und der Glaube." *Hülfe im Bibelnot* 18. 216–228.

"Schrift, Glaube, Erfahrung." *Neue Christoterpe* 17. (1896) 1–11.

"J.T. Becks theologische Arbeit." *Beiträge zur Forderung christlicher Theologie* 8. vol. 4 (1904) 25–46.

"Atheistische Methoden in der Theologie." *Beiträge* 9. vol. 5 (1905).

"Der Zweifel an der Messianität Jesu." *Beiträge* 11. vol. 4 (1907).

"Die Bedeutung der Methode für die theologische Arbeit", *Theologische Literaturbericht* 31. #1 (Jan. 1908) 5–8.

"Die Theologie des Neuen Testaments und die Dogmatik." *Beiträge* 13. ৵ 2 (1909). Trans. by Robert Morgan in *The Nature of New Testament Theology.*

"Der Glaube und die Geschichte." *Gesunde Lehre.* 26.

"Karl Barths Römerbrief. Zweite Aufl. in neuer Bearbeitung 1922." *Furche* 12. vol. 6 (March 1922) 228–232. English translation by James Robinson in *The Beginnings of Dialectical Theology.* ed. James Robinson.

"Natur, Sünde und Gnade." *Gesunde Lehre* 5. 49–68.

"Das Ziel der Geschichte." *Gesunde Lehre* 27. 350–355.

Secondary Sources

Major works:

Bailer, Albert. *Das Systematische Prinzip in der Theologie Adolf Schlatters.* Arbeiten zur Theologie, II. Reihe 12. Stuttgart: Calwer Verlag, 1968.

Bockmühl, Klaus. ed., *Die Aktualität der Theologie Adolf Schlatters*.
    Giessen/Basel: Brunnen Verlag, 1988.
    Contributors: (in order of presentation)
    –Burkhardt, Helmut. "Kann Theologie Wissenschaft sein?"
    –Riesner, Rainer. "Adolf Schlatter und die Geschichte des
        Judenchristentums Jerusalem."
    –Neuer, Werner. "Die ökumenische Bedeutung des Theologie Adolf
        Schlatters."
    –Bockmühl, Klaus. "Die Wahrnehmung die Geschichte in der
        Dogmatik Adolf Schlatters."
    –Bittner, Wolfgang J. "Methodische Grundentscheide in der
        exegetischen Arbeit Adolf Schlatters am Beispiel seiner
        Schriften zum Johannes-Evangelium."

Egg, Gerhard. *Adolf Schlatters Kritische Position, gezeigt an seiner
    Matthäusinterpretation*. Arbeiten zur Theologie, II. Reihe 14.
    Stuttgart: Calwer Verlag, 1968.

Kindt, Irmgard. *Der Gedanke der Einheit: Adolf Schlatters Theologie und
    ihre historischen Voraussetungen*. Stuttgart: Calwer Verlag, 1978.

Luck, Ulrich. *Kerygma und Tradition in der Hermeneutik Adolf
    Schlatters*. Arbeitsgemeinschaft für Forschung des Landes
    Nordrhein-Westfalen 45, 1955.

Neuer, Werner. *Adolf Schlatter*. Wuppertal: R. Brockhaus Verlag,
    1988.

Neuer, Werner. *Dogmatik und Ethik bei Adolf Schlatter*.
    Giessen\Basel: Brunnen Verlag, 1986.

Schmid, Johnannes Heinrich. *Erkenntnis des geschichtlichen Christus bei
    Martin Kähler und bei Adolf Schlatter*. Theologische Zeitschrift,
    Sonderband V. Basel: Friedrich Reinhardt Verlag, 1978.

Articles:

Althaus, P. "Adolf Schlatters Gabe an die systematische Theologie."
    Deutsche Theologie 5 (1938): 146–153.

Bultmann, R. "Rezension von A. Schlatters 'Theologie des Neuen Testaments'." in *Monatschrift für Pastoral Theologie* 8 (1912): 440–443.

Delling, G. "Adolf Schlatters Hermeneutik." *Evangelisch-Lutherische Kirchenzeitung* 6 (1952): 300–303.

Grützmacher, R. "Rezension von A. Schlatters 'Das Christliche Dogma'." *Neue Kirchliche Zeitschrift* 22 (1911): 839–872.

Güting, E. "Zu den Voraussetzungen des systematischen Denkens Adolf Schlatters." *Neue Zeitschrift für Systematische Theologie* 15 (1973): 132–147.

Heim, K. "Offener Brief an Prof. A. Schlatter." *Monatschrift für Pastoral Theologie* 28 (1932): 67–79.

Köberle, A. "Adolf Schlatter als systematischer Theologe." *FAuB* 6 (1952): 239–248.

Leuenberger, R. "Adolf Schlatter und die 'atheistische Methoden in der Theologie'." *Reformatio* 15 (1966): 291–299.

Luck, U. "Adolf Schlatter", *Religion in Geschichte und Gegenwart* 3, Bh V, 1420f.

Lütgert, W. "A. Schlatter als Theologe innerhalb des geistigen Lebens seiner Zeit." *Beiträge zur Forderung christlicher Theologie* 37 (1932) 5–52.

Michel, O. "Adolf Schlatter als Ausleger der Heiligen Schrift." *FAuB* 6 (1952): 227–238.

Neuer, Werner. "Adolf Schlatter (1852–1938): Bahnbrecher eines biblisch-theologischen Realismus." pp. 185–202 in, *Gegen die Gottvergessenheit: Schweizer Theologen im 19. und 20. Jahrhundert,* ed. by Stephan Leimgruber and Max Schloch (Herder: Basel, 1990).

Smidt, U. "'Natürliche Theologie'–als Problem bei Adolf Schlatter." *Evangelische Theologie Heft* 3 (1952): 105–120.

Stuhlmacher, Peter. "Adolf Schlatter als Paulusausleger–ein Versuch." *Theologische Beiträge* (August 1989): 176–190.

Wendland, H.D. "Adolf Schlatters Fragen an die Theologie." *Evangelisch–Lutherische Kirchenzeitung* (1952): 315–317.

Werner, M. "Adolf Schlatter als Dogmatiker." *SThU* 22 (1952): 121–126.

Wernle, P. "Von einer neuen positiven Dogmatik. Rezension von Adolf Schlatter, 'Das Christliche Dogma'." *Christliche Welt* 26 (1912): 15–21.